Warington W. (Warington Wilkinson) Smyth

Coal and coal-mining

Warington W. (Warington Wilkinson) Smyth

Coal and coal-mining

ISBN/EAN: 9783743319608

Manufactured in Europe, USA, Canada, Australia, Japa

Cover: Foto ©ninafisch / pixelio.de

Manufactured and distributed by brebook publishing software (www.brebook.com)

Warington W. (Warington Wilkinson) Smyth

Coal and coal-mining

PREFACE

This handbook is addressed to engineers. It should be of use to inventors and manufacturers generally. It is not a treatise on the patent law. It is not a textbook; it is a handbook.

The engineer is not only the moving power in American industry, but he is coming to be the the Yankee inventor raised to the nth power. As a scientist, he begins where the untrained thinker leaves off. He knows that the pot of gold is not at the foot of a rainbow, but at the end of a long, straight road of sustained scientific effort.

The need of such a handbook as this has become evident in many ways, and has been given emphasis in connection with informal talks to the students in engineering in Sibley College during the periods of my regular lectures on patent law before the Cornell University College of Law. The final word which set my pen going came from him to whom this book is inscribed.

Departing from the orthodox order of the works on patent law and omitting legal phraseology and

PREFACE

terminology to the utmost, I have endeavored to state in plain words those things which the inventor, the industrial leader, and especially the engineer, want to know. The paragraphing and indexing has been given special attention, with a view to making the contents accessible with the utmost directness. The footnotes are not at all a collection of the authorities; but rather typical and illustrative cases which serve as guideboards to further study of many subjects.

WILLIAM MACOMBER.

BUFFALO,
   September, 1912.

TABLE OF CONTENTS

PAGE

References and Abbreviations xvii

CHAPTER I
INTRODUCTORY

§ 1. The Passing of the Old Inventor	1
§ 2. Large Attainments Required	2
§ 3. Relation of the Engineer to Patents . . .	3
§ 4. Relation of Engineer and Patent Attorney . .	5
§ 5. General Knowledge of the Patent Law Necessary	6
§ 6. Supremacy of Our System of Patent Law . .	8
§ 7. Its Service, Faults, and Dangers	11
§ 8. Survey of the Field of Discussion	13

CHAPTER II
WHAT IS A PATENT?

§ 9. General Statement	20
§ 10. The Patent a Pure Monopoly	25
§ 11. The Contract Theory	26
§ 12. The Facts *versus* Theories	27
§ 13. The Constitutional Source of the Patent Laws .	28
§ 14. The Patent Laws	29
§ 15. The Pivotal Act — R. S., § 4886	30

CONTENTS

CHAPTER III

THE NATURE OF INVENTION

		PAGE
§ 16.	Patentable Invention	32
§ 17.	Invention as a Pure Mental Act	33
§ 18.	The Twofold Character of Invention	36
§ 19.	Reduction to Practice	42
§ 20.	Invention and Mechanical Skill	44
§ 21.	Some General Rules	46

CHAPTER IV

WHAT IS PATENTABLE

§ 22.	Introductory Statements	48
§ 23.	A Machine	50
§ 24.	A Manufacture or Composition of Matter	54
§ 25.	An Art or Process	59
§ 26.	An Improvement	63
§ 27.	A Design	64
§ 28.	Summary of these Classes	67
§ 29.	Things not Patentable	68
	¶ 1. Mental Conception	68
	¶ 2. A Force of Nature	69
	¶ 3. Scientific Principles	70
	¶ 4. Property of Matter	71
	¶ 5. Result or Function	71
	¶ 6. Aggregation	72
	¶ 7. Duplication	73
	¶ 8. Simplification	73
	¶ 9. Double Use or Analogous Use	74
	¶ 10. Transposition of Parts	76
	¶ 11. Immoral Object	76
§ 30.	Things Generally Nonpatentable	76
	¶ 1. Adaptation	78
	¶ 2. Carrying Forward	79
	¶ 3. Change of Form	80
	¶ 4. Substitution	80
	¶ 5. Systems and Arrangements	81
	¶ 6. Tests of these Classes	81

CONTENTS

CHAPTER V

PATENTABLE NOVELTY

	PAGE
§ 31. Novelty a Statutory Requirement	83
§ 32. Things which defeat Patentable Novelty . .	85
¶ 1. Prior Knowledge of or Use by Others in This Country before Invention	85
¶ 2. Prior Patent or Publication in any Country (1) Before the Inventive Act, (2) More than Two Years before Application . .	87
¶ 3. Public Use or Sale more than Two Years in this Country	88
¶ 4. Abandonment	89
§ 33. Generic Invention and Improvements . . .	90
§ 34. Evidence and Tests of Novelty	92
¶ 1. Patent Office Action and the Patent Itself .	92
¶ 2. Public Acquiescence	93
¶ 3. Commercial Success and Extensive Use .	93
¶ 4. Efficiency and Utility	94
¶ 5. Prior Failures — Last Step Rule . . .	96
¶ 6. Extensive Litigation	97
¶ 7. Attempted Evasion	98
¶ 8. Use by Defendant	98

CHAPTER VI

THE OBTAINING OF PATENTS

§ 35. Introductory	100
§ 36. Attorneys and Solicitors	101
§ 37. Selecting a Patent Attorney	103
§ 38. When Application should be Filed	105
§ 39. Searches and Preliminary Examinations . .	110
§ 40. Preparing a Case for the Patent Attorney . .	112
§ 41. The Parts of the Application	113
¶ 1. The Petition	114
¶ 2. The Power of Attorney	114
¶ 3. The Specification	115
¶ 4. The Claims	116

CONTENTS

	PAGE
¶ 5. The Oath	116
¶ 6. The Drawings	117
§ 42. Examination	118
§ 43. The First Action	119
§ 44. Amendment or Argument after First Action	123
§ 45. Subsequent Actions and Amendments	125
§ 46. Interferences	127
§ 47. Allowance and Issue	128
§ 48. Abandoned and Forfeited Applications	130
§ 49. Application by Executor, Administrator, or Committee	131
§ 50. Disclaimer	131
§ 51. Reissues	133
§ 52. Foreign Patents	136

CHAPTER VII

CLAIM CONSTRUCTION

§ 53. General Statements	139
§ 54. Statutory Provision	141
§ 55. General Rules of Patent Construction	143
§ 56. Plain Intent and Meaning	144
§ 57. Analysis of Claim	145
§ 58. Combinations	151
§ 59. Reference to Specifications and Drawings	152
§ 60. Beneficial Uses	153
§ 61. Generic Inventions and Specific Improvements	154
§ 62. Equivalents	156
§ 63. Dissecting Claims	159
§ 64. Limitation of Claim	160
¶ 1. The Prior Art	160
¶ 2. By Terms of Application	163
¶ 3. By Patent Office Action	164
¶ 4. By Reference Characters	165
¶ 5. By Words of Limitation	166
¶ 6. Omitting Element — Unclaimed Element	167
¶ 7. By Disclaimer or Reissue	168

CONTENTS

	PAGE
§ 65. Construction with Reference to Anticipation	168
¶ 1. Ex Post Facto Judgment	169
¶ 2. Prior Public Use	170
¶ 3. Analogous or Nonanalogous Use	172
¶ 4. Abandoned Device or Experiment	173
¶ 5. Inoperative Device	174
¶ 6. Foreign Use	175
¶ 7. Prior Domestic Patent	176
¶ 8. Prior Publication	177
¶ 9. Prior Foreign Patent	179
¶ 10. Infringe-if-Later Test	179
§ 66. Construction with Reference to Infringement	180
¶ 1. Combinations	181
¶ 2. Process	183
¶ 3. Valeat quam Pereat Rule	184
¶ 4. Repairing and Rebuilding	185
§ 67. The Province of the Expert	186

CHAPTER VIII

INFRINGEMENT

§ 68. General Statement and the Statute	189
§ 69. Who May Commit Infringement?	190
¶ 1. Joint Owners	190
¶ 2. Licensor and Licensee	191
¶ 3. Copartners	191
¶ 4. Assignor and Assignee	192
¶ 5. Corporations	192
¶ 6. Employer and Employee	193
¶ 7. Intent — Ignorance	194
§ 70. As to the Nature of the Act	194
¶ 1. Contributory Infringement	195
¶ 2. Importation	197
¶ 3. Territorial Rights	198
¶ 4. Buying a Machine without the Right to Use	198
§ 71. Infringement of the Different Classes of Patentable Invention	199
¶ 1. Art or Process	200

CONTENTS

		PAGE
¶ 2.	A Machine	200
¶ 3.	Machine and Manufacture	201
¶ 4.	Manufacture or Composition of Matter	201
¶ 5.	Improvements	203
¶ 6.	Designs	203
§ 72.	Some General Observations	204

CHAPTER IX
PATENT LITIGATION

§ 73.	General View of the Subject	206
§ 74.	Wrongs Against Unpatented Inventions	208
§ 75.	Wrongs Affecting Property Rights in Inventions	212
§ 76.	Wrongs Against Patented Inventions	212
§ 77.	The Geography of an Equity Action	217
§ 78.	Defenses in an Action for Infringement	225
	¶ 1. Fraud or Misrepresentation in the Specification	225
	¶ 2. Fraud or Unfairness Against another Inventor	226
	¶ 3. Anticipation	226
	¶ 4. Noninventorship	227
	¶ 5. Public Use or Abandonment	228
	¶ 6. Nonpatentability	230
	¶ 7. Noninvention	230
	¶ 8. Joint Invention Patented to a Sole Applicant or a Sole Invention Patented to Joint Applicants	230
	¶ 9. License — Release — Estoppel	231
	¶ 10. Defense of Not Guilty	232
	¶ 11. Other Defenses	233
§ 79.	Preliminary Injunctions	234
§ 80.	Damages and Profits	240

CHAPTER X
PROPERTY RIGHTS

§ 81.	Introductory	241
§ 82.	The Three States or Conditions	243

CONTENTS

		PAGE
83.	Future Inventions	244
84.	Unpatented Inventions	247
85.	Patented Inventions	248
86.	The Three Divisions of Interest	249
	¶ 1. Common Tenancy	249
	¶ 2. Territorial Assignments or Grants	251
	¶ 3. Tenancy by the Entirety — Trust Holdings	253
87.	Assignments	254
88.	Recording Assignments	256
89.	Matters Concerning Assignments	258
	¶ 1. Unconditional Assignments	258

REFERENCES AND ABBREVIATIONS

R. S. or *U. S. R. S.* refer to U. S. Revised Statutes.

U. S. refers to United States Supreme Court Reports.

L. Ed. refers to the Lawyers' Edition of those reports.

S. Ct. refers to West Publishing Co. edition of those reports.

Cranch
Wheat.
Pet. refer to the several reporters of the U. S. Supreme
How.   Court Reports.
Wall.

C. C. A. refers to the Circuit Court of Appeals Reports, which contain the decisions of the nine circuit courts of appeals.

Fed. refers to the Federal Reporter, which contains the same decisions as the C. C. A. Reports, and also the decisions of the Federal Circuit and District courts.

O. G. refers to the Patent Office Gazette, in which are found many court decisions and all Patent Office decisions.

Rob. Pat. refers to Robinson on Patents.

Walk. Pat. refers to Walker on Patents.

Mac. Pat. refers to Macomber, "The Fixed Law of Patents," Second Edition.

P. O. Rules refer, respectively, to Rules of Practice in the
Pat. Stat.   United States Patent Office, and the Patent Laws, both pamphlets published by the Patent Office, which may be had gratis by addressing the Commissioner of Patents, Washington, D. C.

CHAPTER I

INTRODUCTORY

§ 1. The Passing of the Old Inventor

THE time was when the American inventor was merely a clever Yankee. He could sit and whittle and whistle, and in due time produce something patentable. The clever Yankee and his day are history. Great engineering schools have come; they are everywhere, big and little. In almost any village with but a single industry may be found a trained engineer such as McCormick could not have found in 1850 to develop his reaper had he searched two continents. Any one of our five hundred colleges is turning out yearly chemists who know more of analysis and synthesis than all the chemists Goodyear could have found in 1839, when he discovered, by accident, the process of vulcanizing rubber. The inventor of to-day begins leagues upon leagues beyond where the New England Yankee ended. In another decade it will be nearly the whole truth to say that the American inventor is the trained engineer and chemist.

When we come to consider invention in its psychological aspect we shall see why the inventor of the future must be, as a rule, a man of high scientific training.

§ 2. Large Attainments Required

But it must be noted here that this change is not only a question of quality, but, in a sense, one of quantity as well. More than a million patents have been granted by our Federal Government. These alone constitute a mass of knowledge and discovery beyond the power of any one man to master; and they are but an element of the sum total of the known. Since true invention begins where the known ends, it is evident that, before any man may even enter upon the larger fields of important invention, he must possess an enormous mass of complex and difficult knowledge — else he wanders aimlessly in a field unknown to him but known to others, and invents over and over things long since invented, patented, and found useful or worthless, as the case may be. This is illustrated by the fact that little more than 50 per cent of the applications for patents in any year mature into grants — probably 40 per cent of all applications being cases of inventing over or reinventing.[1]

§ 3. Relation of the Engineer to Patents

With this new era has come a relation of the engineer to patents not generally appreciated and often misapprehended. There is a natural tendency on the part of many engineers to rather look down upon a patent and upon the patent system as something obsolete along with the Yankee genius who whistled trivialities out of the unknown. There is just reason for so regarding the great mass of microscopic patents which are issued — so microscopic that they slip through the sieve of the Patent Office — but the drawing of a general conclusion and the forming of a general attitude therefrom is quite unwarranted for these reasons:

---

[1] For example, in 1910, 64,448 original applications were filed. In that year 35,930 patents issued. While this does not mean that 28,518 of those applications were refused, it shows that, relatively speaking and in the long run, only a little more than 50 per cent of all applications ever mature into patents; and, of course, the great bulk of these failures is due to want of novelty.

First, as has been noted, the field of activity for real and substantial invention has passed largely into the engineering field — becoming a substantial part of it.

Second, the engineer must, perforce, deal with patent problems as they stand related to engineering and manufacture. The engineer may scorn a patent, scorn the idea of being an inventor; but that does not alter the fact that his client or his concern has to come in contact with the inventions and patents of others. He cannot avoid the condition or the fact; and it is his business to see that his client or his concern does not become involved in infringement or other patent troubles. He has no choice; he must know about patents and know something of the patent law, else he is not qualified for full duty and is not fully caring for the interests intrusted to him.

Third, it is only in comparatively rare instances at the present time that a single patent or even a series of patents constitutes the sole basis of a large enterprise.[1] They constitute, rather,

---

[1] For example, such great concerns as the Edison, Westinghouse, and Western Electric companies would continue

certain protections and advantages which are valuable, but not vital, to the enterprise. The enterprise does not stand or fall with its patents, but, none the less, its improvements and its patents are contributing factors in the earning of profits or dividends which the engineer has no more right to despise or neglect than any other factor contributing to success.

§ 4. Relation of Engineer and Patent Attorney

Then there are some engineers — few in number — who presume to know all about patents and the patent law. They are few in number, just as the patent attorneys who think they know all about engineering are few. The engineer or the patent attorney who knows all in his own calling is yet to be born. The growth of the two sciences limits each to his own field, and at the

in profitable business if all their patent protection were removed; and many instances might be cited where a single patent has been foundational in establishing a large concern which has gone on successfully after the patent has expired.

There is an instance within my own experience where an engineer of national reputation took the view that a patent was something beneath him and refused to protect his own improvements. In due time one of those improvements became of great value. He changed his mind and undertook to secure a patent; but he was too late. Time had made it public property.

same time develops an interdependence between them. To illustrate: Twenty-five years ago I solicited patents upon early types of electrical machinery with comparatively little aid from engineers. It goes without saying that I could not now handle the intricate problems of that art without substantial coöperation of able engineers. And while the engineer of twenty-five years ago could readily point out patentable difference, or infringement or non-infringement of those early machines, the engineer of to-day who would undertake to apply the refined and complex rules of law to determine those questions without the aid of an attorney would be in very deep water.

Thus there has grown up an interdependence and a spirit and habit of coöperation between engineer and patent attorney, with the result that each does his own work better, and by team work accomplishes results neither could attain alone.

§ 5. General Knowledge of the Patent Law Necessary

Consequent upon these conditions, a general knowledge of the patent law becomes necessary to the engineer. Not only must he have such general knowledge to coöperate successfully, but he must have such knowledge to know when to call in the patent attorney.[1] It is the experience of all patent attorneys who have come in contact with numerous problems that a large proportion of patent litigation might have been avoided and many lost inventions saved if the engineer or other person in charge had known enough of the law of patents to realize that a patent problem existed. The real engineer both produces and saves, and often the saving is as important as the producing. It is as much his business to save his client or concern from loss through needless patent litigation or loss of patent rights as it is to save loss of material or labor. Just as preventive medicine is the great and growing power in conserving human life, so preventive engineering must play a larger and larger part in the conservation of industry. The engineer must keep his business healthy and growing, and

[1] The question is often asked: What textbook can I read to secure a general, working knowledge of the patent law? My answer is, read Robinson. When one has become familiar with the general principles as taught by Robinson, my work on The Fixed Law of Patents becomes useful as showing the application of general rules by the appellate courts.

to do so he must know, among other things, the fundamentals of the patent law; and he must employ his patent attorney, as we are coming to employ physicians — to prevent, rather than cure.

§ 6. Supremacy of Our System of Patent Law

It is nothing short of remarkable that those men who wrote the Constitution should have laid a foundation ample for the needs of our patent system for all time. It is hardly less remarkable that Congress — long prior to the present era of industrial development—should have enacted laws which have required little change to meet the expansion and growth of the past half century.

Our patent system, our patent office and our patent laws are the best in the world. Up to 1850 less than a thousand patents had been issued. Patent No. 1,000,000 was issued in August, 1911. In that year 35,930 patents were issued. America produces more inventions than France, Germany and Great Britain combined. Go over the field of invention from Franklin with his toggle-joint press of 1725 down to the automobile harvester of 1911 and see how the United States first forged to the front and finally fairly forestalled the rest of the world in the field of invention.

The statute of 1793 intrusted the granting of patents exclusively to the Attorney-General, the Secretary of State and the Secretary of War — any two of whom could grant a patent over their signatures to any one who reasonably satisfied them that he had a new and useful invention. There was no system by which the inventor or the grantors could possibly know whether the thing patented was novel.

By the act of 1836 the Patent Office was established and a commissioner of patents appointed, and the present system was begun. But it must not be assumed that this early patent office, which was then a bureau of the State Department, was more than a beginning. In 1849 it was made a part of the Department of the Interior, where it has since remained.[1]

The original powers of the commissioner of patents have been enlarged from a mere clerical state to a high judicial position. And with the growth of the office and the powers of its head, there has come a staff of examiners of training,

[1] For history and growth of Patent Office see 12 O. G. 589.

skill and character in no respect inferior to the judiciary which administers our laws.[1]

It is true that, in past time, the office of commissioner was made a stepping-stone to a patent practice, and engendered the fancied idea of a pull or special privilege. So far as I know, there is but one living ex-commissioner obsessed by that fancy.

There has been much gossip — but little written or printed — concerning leaks and crookedness in the Patent Office. So long as commissioners and examiners come and go there will be some leakage; and once in a while one thinks he discovers " an underground railway "[2] with one terminal in the Patent Office. No doubt such have been; and it would be exceeding strange if, with underpaid examiners and wealthy and unscrupulous corporations, leaks and crookedness did not continue. But I am of opinion there is less leakage, less crookedness, than in any other department of the Government. For the few ex-commissioners and ex-examiners who attempt to trade upon

---

[1] See Mac. Pat. §§ 258–263, 783–787.
[2] See Telephone Cases, 126 U. S. 1, 567–8; 31 L. Ed. 863, 1000–1001; 8 S. Ct. 778.

their former official positions both the public and the Patent Office have the proper contempt.

With the development of office, system and established law and with the spread of technical training, invention and patents have ceased to be provincial. But a little time ago New England led in invention. To-day the geographical patent center is out in Ohio, following the center of population; while Massachusetts has fallen to fourth place among the states and California has risen next to her — to fifth place — in the number of patent applications filed per annum. These are significant facts to the engineer; for, go where he may, he will find inventors and patents. And it is the engineer who is largely responsible for this progress; for, as has been said, he is rapidly becoming the real inventor.

§ 7. Its Service, Faults and Dangers

The immeasurable benefits of our patent system need not be dwelt upon; they are self-evident to any unbiased mind. Not only has our patent system been a tremendous factor in our industrial development, but it has been — indirectly, but none the less powerfully — dynamic in the progress of engineering and our great engineering schools. Inventive genius, protected by patents, has been a constant stimulus to industry; industry has demanded engineers; the demand for engineers has begotten the demand for great technical schools. And now these great schools are producing the great inventors who, in turn, will further augment industry, increasing the demand for greater engineers, and greater engineers creating a further demand for greater technical schools. It seems to be an ascending spiral, the end of which is beyond our sight.

Faults there are in our patent system, faults which work wrongs and losses; but that is true of any human institution. The gravest fault is identical with that of our legal system generally — the fault of an archaic system of procedure and a mass of contradictory, hair-splitting case law. The first great step toward reform has just been taken by the Supreme Court in revising the ancient rules which governed the trial of patent causes.[1]

[1] A great lawyer once said, "There, my son, are the reports of the Court of Appeals of the State of New York. In them you can find the law upon any subject and on both sides of the subject." After twenty-five years' experience I am disposed to believe one might point to the Patent Office decisions with a similar remark. I refer to this condition because it is my

Dangers from our patent system are largely imaginary, aside from the outrageous abuses which have been practiced by certain great monopolies. But these dangers grow out of economic, political and legal conditions which are no more chargeable primarily to our patent system than to many other factors which enter in to create unlawful monopoly. The one great danger here arising is that, in the reform which is inevitable, the evils will be wiped out and we shall fly to others we know not of — that there will follow drastic legislation which will cripple true patent industry and legitimate patent monopoly.[1]

§ 8. Survey of the Field of Discussion

As stated in the preface, this is not a textbook on patents. It is an attempt to give prac-

belief that the time is not far when much of these evils will be cured by codical legislation.

[1] The decision of the Supreme Court in the Mimeograph Case (Henry *v.* Dick, 224 U. S. 1; 56 L. Ed. 645; 32 S. Ct. 364) and the wide discussion of Chief Justice White's dissenting opinion therein has led to the introduction of bills in Congress of drastic nature, and is likely to eventuate in legislation far too reactionary. The real evil lies farther back, and should begin with the Harrow Case (Bement *v.* National, 186 U. S. 70; 46 L. Ed. 1058; 22 S. Ct. 747), where the Supreme Court practically exempted the patent privilege from the legitimate workings of antitrust and antimonopoly legislation.

tical answer to four broad questions which the engineer is asking and to shed light upon five problems daily confronting him. These are:

1. What is a patent?
2. What is invention?
3. What is patentable?
4. What is novelty?
5. The problem of obtaining a good patent,
6. The problem of knowing what a patent covers,
7. The problem of infringement,
8. The problem of patent litigation,
9. The problem of property rights in patents.

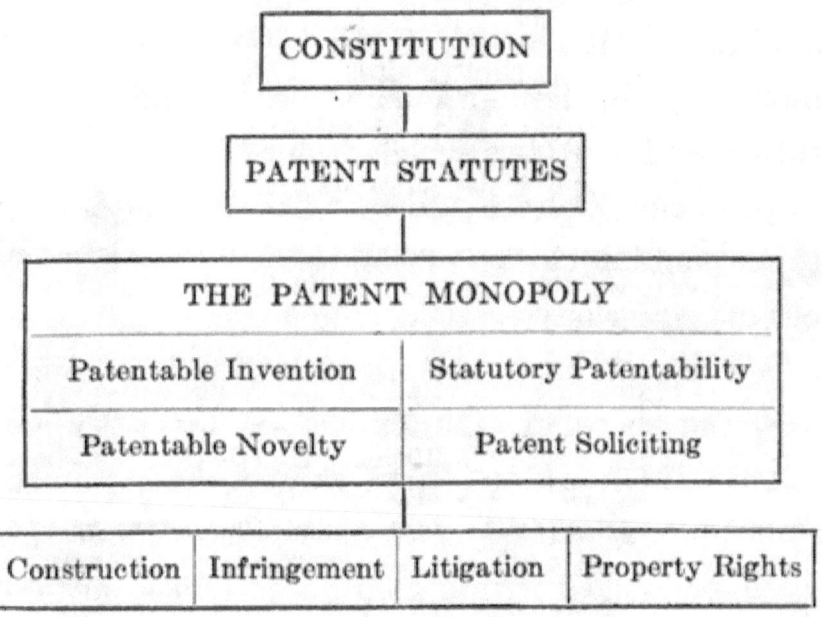

Should we attempt to diagram the subject — while such a subject does not yield itself readily to graphic representation — it would appear substantially as shown on the preceding page.

Growing out of the Constitution is the patent statute. Under this statute the monopoly is created. The grant of the monopoly is dependent upon four conditions: patentable invention, statutory patentability, patentable novelty and the proper application for a grant and its prosecution. The patent monopoly thus created gives rise to four further considerations — construction, infringement, litigation, and property rights.

Accordingly, we first ask the question, what is a patent? We note its character as a limited monopoly, its foundation in the Federal Constitution and the laws which Congress has enacted in obedience thereto and its nature as a contract to promote progress rather than as a monopoly of odious nature.

Second, finding that invention and discovery may thus be made the subject of a limited monopoly, the question is self-asking, what is invention and discovery? In answering this question we have to deal with a mental act and a physical act; and we also have to differentiate the inventor from the mechanic — the one who creates and the other who adapts that which is already created.

Third, there comes the question, is everything one may invent or discover patentable? Could the Wright Brothers have patented the art of human flight? Could Peary have patented the discovery of the North Pole? Here we turn to constitution and statute to find that patentable invention or discovery is strictly limited, and endeavor to mark these limitations. And in so doing we discover that there are numerous things or acts distinctly nonpatentable, and some things or acts which may or may not be patentable, according to various circumstances and conditions.

Fourth, in attempting to answer these three questions we have raised another — what is novelty? It is plain from the statute that novelty is an absolute prerequisite to patentability, and it is also evident that numerous things operate to defeat novelty; but by far the largest problem here is to know how to determine when actual novelty is present. To solve this problem the courts have evolved certain tests which are of large use to the engineer.

Long before reaching this point it has been discovered that there are good patents and worthless patents; and the first of the five problems is how to secure a good patent. Here must be considered what sort of a man one should employ to supervise so important an undertaking. Moreover, it appears that the engineer must coöperate with the attorney, and, therefore, he must know somewhat of the great machine in Washington which grinds the grist of American invention.

In this review of Patent Office procedure it is found that the claim is the vital thing in a patent, and a most difficult question is what the patent covers, what it protects, what must be avoided. Hence we find that the courts have elaborated principles, rules and tests which the engineer may use to great advantage in marking the boundaries of a patent in order to determine what he or another may or may not do.

There is an old saying that no man can so live but that he may be sued, but any man may so live that he cannot have the judgment of a court against him. No engineer can conduct a business so that it may not be sued for infringement, but he may so conduct his business that a charge of infringement cannot succeed. This is our third problem. To keep the law one must know the law; and so, in this chapter, some of the rocks and shoals are pointed out to the end that the engineer may pilot his craft safely.

But there are conditions under which war is inevitable; neither careful conduct nor preparedness can avoid it. At times the engineer must defend his concern against suit for infringement; at other times he must protect it by aggressive action against infringers of its patent monopoly. It is essential, therefore, that he should know the general course and trend of patent litigation; know the mighty power of an injunction; know under what circumstances damages and profits may be adjudged; know whether his cause is being prosecuted vigorously and speedily. Only the peaks of this subject are touched; it is far too large for thorough treatment.

Finally there comes the problem of property rights in patents. A patent is a peculiar kind of property, and, necessarily, it is subject to rules peculiar to it. Since this is a subject of most vital concern to the engineer, it is given, perhaps, more than its just share of space in this handbook. The three states or conditions—future inventions, unpatented inventions and patented inventions—present their respective problems. The three divisions of interest — common tenancy, territorial rights and tenancy by the entirety — present theirs. The various kinds of assignments, licenses and shop rights call out problems of their own.

It is a large field for a small book; but knowing that one of the best of histories of the United States is a small volume written by an Irishman who never saw America, we will approach the subject at least hopefully.

CHAPTER II

WHAT IS A PATENT?

§ 9. General Statement

WHAT is a patent? This may seem a kindergarten question, but the utter lack of any exact ideas even on the part of men of more than ordinary intelligence, and the grotesquely distorted ideas of many warrant its asking.[1]

In the first place, the right to a patent is not a

---

[1] The meaning of the words "patent" and "patented" as used in sec. 4887 is not difficult to ascertain. The word "patent," originally a qualifying adjective applied to the "open letters" by which a sovereign grants an estate or privilege, has come to mean, in connection with the so-called patent laws of the United States, as well as in common parlance, the exclusive privilege itself granted by the sovereign authority to the inventor with respect to his invention. What the nature and extent of the exclusive privilege thus granted by the Constitution and the laws of the United States may be, depends upon the terms of the act of Congress providing for and regulating the same; and when this section 4887 speaks of an invention which has been previously patented in a foreign country, it obviously means an invention with respect to which the inventor has received from the sovereign authority of such country such exclusive privilege as its laws provide for and sanction. — Atlas v. Simonds, 102 Fed. 643; 42 C. C. A. 398.

natural right. It is a right created by Congress in pursuance of the authority given by the Constitution. As will be seen later, it is a right limited to certain things and limited to very definite conditions. A patent is a document " issued in the name of the United States of America, and shall be signed by the Commissioner of Patents, and they shall be recorded, together with the specifications, in the Patent Office in books to be kept for that purpose." (R. S. 4883). This document contains the description and drawings, if there are drawings, and claims, which latter specify, limit and define exactly what has been found, after examination of the prior art by the Patent Office, to be novel and patentable.

This document gives to the patentee, his executors, administrators or assigns, the exclusive right to make, use and sell the described and claimed invention throughout the United States and the Territories thereof.[1]

---

[1] The authority by which the patent issues is that of the United States of America. The seal which is used is the seal of the Patent Office, and that was created by congressional enactment. It is signed by the Secretary of the Interior, and the Commissioner of Patents, who also countersigns it, is an officer of that department. The patent, then, is not the exercise of any prerogative power or discretion of the

But, it may be asked, would not the inventor have the right to make, use and sell his invention if he did not have a patent? Certainly, and so would every one else. That is just the point. The patent does not give you any more right to make, or use, or sell than you had before; but it gives you the right for seventeen years *to prevent any one else from using your invention*, either by making, using, or selling without your consent. A patent is not a license; it is rather a club. It gives you the right to go into court, show your monopoly, show that it has been invaded, and invoke the strong arm of the law to make the infringer stop — stop making, stop using, stop selling your patented invention. And you must know that there is no power in the United States so great as that of a court of equity when it exercises its power to order an injunction; for back of that power lies the entire police power of the nation, including, if need be, the army and navy;

President, or by any other officer of the Government, but is the result of a course of proceeding, quasi judicial in character, and is not subject to be repealed or revoked by the President, the Secretary of the Interior, or by the Commissioner of Patents, when once issued. — U. S. *v.* Am. Bell Tel. 128 U. S. 315; 32 L. Ed. 450; 9 S. Ct. 90.

and the Federal courts will resent any infraction of this sacred and high power with penalty of fine and incarceration.[1]

And this monopoly given you is absolute. No one can even make your invention for his own use, though there is a popular notion to the contrary.[2] No one can use your patented invention without your consent, even if it is given to him. No one can sell such an infringing device merely to get rid of it, except he sells it for junk.[3] Nor do you have to use your invention. This is quite different from the patent laws of most other countries. But under the present law you may lock your patent in a safe, let it gather dust and mold, and pursue a dog-in-the-manger attitude for seventeen years.[4] But, as we shall see later, while

---

[1] The cases declare that he receives nothing from the law that he did not have before, and that the only effect of the patent is to restrain others from manufacturing and using that which he has patented. Whenever this court has had occasion to speak, it has decided that an inventor receives from a patent the right to exclude others from its use for the time prescribed by the statute. — Continental v. Eastern, 210 U. S. 405; 52 L. Ed. 1122; 28 S. Ct. 748.

[2] Rob. Pat. § 946.

[3] Henry v. Dick, 224 U. S. 1; 56 L. Ed. 645; 32 S. Ct. 364.

[4] Heaton v. Eureka, 77 Fed. 288; 25 C. C. A. 267; Draper v. American, 161 Fed. 728; 88 C. C. A. 588; Lewis v. Premium, 163 Fed. 950, 90 C. C. A. 310.

you may pursue this course and still be able to stop infringement at the end of a litigation, the courts are slow to grant you immediate relief by injunction, and still slower to award you damages upon a patent which has been kept in cold storage the years that it should have been of service to mankind.

So you have a monopoly absolute for a given time; which you can enforce by the strongest arm of the Federal Government; and which dies at the end of seventeen years, absolutely and without possible right of renewal or extension.

And we shall see, as we proceed, that such a monopoly must be construed and interpreted with care, in order that it may not become a block to progress, or cover more than the patentee actually invented; for as Justice Shiras said: "A pioneer patent does not shut, but opens, the door for subsequent invention."[1] And if this is true of a pioneer patent, it is true of an improvement or minor patent. So the Patent Office and the courts, under the statutes, have surrounded this monopoly with rules and decisions which at once protect it

---

[1] Westinghouse *v.* Boyden, 170 U. S. 537, 574; 42 L. Ed. 1136, 1149; 18 S. Ct. 707.

and at the same time protect the public from unjust use of it.

§ 10. The Patent a Pure Monopoly

During the reigns of Elizabeth and James I, crown monopolies of the necessaries of life became unbearable. By a decision of Lord Coke,[1] it was held that the crown had no right to grant a perpetual monopoly, and this was followed by the Statute of Monopolies which abolished all monopolies save those granted for limited times for inventions. Here was the pure monopoly theory of a patent which came down to us, and which was the theory held by the Supreme Court for many years. It was the theory which that court held when it declared a patent void merely because, through accident, it had failed to receive a signature at the time of issuance.[2] This view made the grant a one-sided affair, to be strictly construed and defeated at all possible points.

[1] Darcey v. Allin, 11 Coke R. 84 b.
[2] Marsh v. Nichols, 128 U. S. 605; 52 L. Ed. 538; 9 S. Ct. 168. But this extreme view has been somewhat modified in later decisions. Western v. North, 135 Fed. 79; 67 C. C. A. 553.

§ 11. The Contract Theory

Then a somewhat wiser opinion came in what is known as the "contract theory."[1] This theory may be paraphrased in this way: The Government and the inventor enter into a contract whereby the Government says to the inventor, 'If you produce a new and useful invention which will add to the wealth, comfort or happiness of the people, and if you will disclose your invention and define it precisely so that the people may use it after your patent has expired, and also what you claim to have invented — no more, no less, — as a reward for your industry and for the addition which you have made to the utilities of life, and for the example of progress you have set, we, the Government, will allow you to enjoy the full fruits of your invention exclusively for a period of seventeen years. During those seventeen years you may invoke the powers of the Federal courts to protect you in this limited mo-

---

[1] It is commonly supposed that this theory was first announced by Justice Miller in the Telephone Cases (126 U. S. 1; 31 L. Ed. 863; 8 S. Ct. 778). True, it gained currency from that time, but at least four years earlier Justice Mattews announced the same theory in Butterworth v. Hoe, 112 U. S. 50; 28 L. Ed. 656; 5 S. Ct. 25.

nopoly; but after the expiration of that period, the public becomes the owner of your discovery.'

§ 12. The Facts *versus* Theories

Here, then, are two theories — the one where the grant is regarded as a pure, one-sided monopoly to be treated with strict construction and all severity; and the other where it is regarded as a contract to be treated under the broad rules of equity, much the same as any other contract. So much for theory; now for the facts: *A patent creates nothing that did not exist before the grant. All that the patent creates is a right bestowed upon the inventor, good during the life of the patent and no longer, to invoke the powers of the courts to maintain the exclusiveness of the monopoly.* A patent creates nothing. Perforce, what it covers must have existed before, else there could be no patent. One might have invented no end of valuable things under the common law, and he could use what he invented; but he could not protect himself in the exclusive enjoyment of the product of his genius; it was common property; there was no monopoly. Hence the second point to be kept in mind: *A patent is a grant in contravention of the common law right.* It is, after all, a monopoly, and must find its justification in constitution and statute. The "contract theory" is a just and proper theory to be used in construing the grant; but it is none the less true that it rests upon statutory enactment, which must root back in the fundamental provision of the Constitution.[1]

§ 13. The Constitutional Source of the Patent Laws

Therefore, the patent laws of the United States have their root and origin in the provision under § 8, Art. 1, of the Federal Constitution, which reads:

"The Congress shall have power, . . .

To promote the progress of science and useful arts by securing for limited times to authors and inventors the exclusive right to their respective writings and discoveries."

The plain content of this provision is that it established a quasi contractual relationship be-

---

[1] The only grant to the patentee was the right to exclude others, to have and to hold for himself and his assigns a monopoly, not a right limited or conditioned according to the sentiment of judges, but an absolute monopoly conferred by the sovereign lawmakers. — Rubber Tire *v.* Milwaukee, 154 Fed. 358; 83 C. C. A. 336. See also Continental *v.* Eastern, 210 U. S. 405; 52 L. Ed. 1122; 28 S. Ct. 748.

tween the Government as the agent of the people and the inventor. It does not make the grant aught else than a monopoly,[1] but it makes the monopoly a limited, legitimate monopoly, and fully justifies the contract theory as a theory useful in interpretation and construction.

§ 14. The Patent Laws

We are not concerned with the history and analysis of these laws, further than to note the fact that this provision of the Constitution gave Congress the power to enact general patent laws and also to grant patents by special act.[2] In early days many patents were granted by special acts, but this practice is long defunct; and it is most improbable that Congress will ever again exercise the privilege.

With the act of 1870 and the amendments of 1871, 1872, and 1874, the patent statute became substantially fixed. A pivot was then established which, with very little truing and adjusting, has been the common center about which our

[1] National v. Interchangeable, 106 Fed. 693; 45 C. C. A. 544.
[2] Evans v. Eaton, 3 Wheat. (16 U. S.) 454; 4 L. Ed. 433; Grant v. Raymond, 6 Pet. (31 U. S.) 218; 8 L. Ed. 376.

entire patent system has turned for nearly half a century with a minimum of friction.[1]

§ 15. The Pivotal Act — R. S., § 4886

By the act of 1870 and by two amendments — one in 1896 and one in 1897 — this pivot was established:

§ 4886. Any person who has invented or discovered any new and useful art, machine, manufacture, or composition of matter, or any new and useful improvements thereof, not known or used by others in this country, before his invention or discovery thereof, and not patented or described in any printed publication in this or any foreign country, before his invention or discovery thereof, or more than two years prior to his application, and not in public use or on sale in this country for more than two years prior to his application, unless the same is proved to have been abandoned, may, upon payment of the fees required by law, and other due proceeding had, obtain a patent therefor.

Patents for designs, which are considered elsewhere, have a pivot of their own under §§ 4929–4933, and are given their special protection.

---

[1] An excellent digest of the subjects covered by the several acts and amendments of Congress will be found under § 48, Rob. Pat.

But however perfect the pivot, the wheel does not turn until power is applied. Section 4886 provides for the creation of the grant, but it does not render it dynamic. Sections 4920 and 4921 turn on the power. They give the United States courts the power to impose damages for trespass upon the rights of the patentee, to issue injunctions to restrain infringement, and to compel accountings for profits. There is a popular idea that a patent is a sort of magician's wand or a stuffed club. A patent creates nothing that did not exist before the grant. Section 4886 merely provides for the granting of patents for specified classes of inventions. If the law stopped there, we should have nothing of value. Sections 4920 and 4921 give the patentee the right to invoke the powers of a Federal court to protect his monopoly; and thus is seen the fact that, after all, a patent is no more and no less than a special warrant to sue for redress for the commission of infringing acts. The invocation and application of these powers will be considered under the several titles of actions and defenses, injunctions, damages and profits.

CHAPTER III

THE NATURE OF INVENTION

§ 16. Patentable Invention

As will be seen later, not all invention is patentable. But what is patentable invention? I once put that question to an expert witness, and he was unwise enough to attempt an answer. At the end of a half day he had produced a clever essay, but a definition of invention — by no means. The courts, from Justice Taney down to the newest district judge with his first patent cause, have attempted a definition. All have failed.[1] And it is needless to say I shall attempt no such task. There are certain phenomena having their origin in that mysterious thing, the human brain, which are incapable of definition. Invention is one of them. We may study its manifestations and characteristics, but define it we never can. And in thus studying it, it is evident that we may ap-

[1] For a collection of attempted definitions of invention and mechanical skill, see Mac. Pat. §§ 614, 656, 657.

proach it as a pure mental act, or as it discloses itself in concrete form. Both will be useful.

§ 17. Invention as a Pure Mental Act

At its foundation, an invention is an idea — as Robinson says, "an idea of means." It is a mental act, a conception, a revelation. The machine, the composition, the design — all are concretions; but the indefinable something which preceded and *caused* each was an activity of the mind, the result of which we call invention.

Let us indulge in a supposition which may be of use and which will also serve to show how and why the inventor is becoming more and more the trained engineer. Suppose I have before me a desired end; I wish to produce a machine which will do a certain thing. What have I to start with? In my conscious mind I have the thing to be done — the function of the machine. In the storehouse of memory — the subconscious portion of the mind — is hidden away all the knowledge I have of mechanical devices, elements, mechanical movements and combinations which may produce certain results. These things are hidden away below the horizon of mental vision, and yet they are there. What I wish to do is to select from this knowledge in the subliminal storehouse the elements I need and put them together so as to give me a *vision* of a machine to accomplish the desired end. The main elements are usually in view, for usually the invention is but an improvement upon something already known. But I want a different combination. How shall I get it? If we say by imagination, we are nearing it; but we have not yet arrived. My imagination pictures various things, but I know they are *not it;* they are something else — aggregations, mechanical skill; I know that, as yet, I have *created* nothing. Suddenly there springs into consciousness the picture of the thing sought. I know, and know instantly, that I have *created* something.

It is said that the desire for food has been the evolutionary cause of the hoof of the reindeer, almost as hard as tempered steel, which will cut through snow and solid ice to the moss beneath, upon which the animal feeds. Perhaps invention is an analogous potentiality. The desire to attain an end, and the thought of it, and the longing for it, create a mental stimulus which sets up a cellular process of combination and recombination and building together of those things stored in the subconscious region until a true combination is made; and then it springs into consciousness.

If this theory is correct, at least two facts follow: First, one can create by invention only that which is a combination of elements or application of forces the elements of which were, in some form, in the storehouse of memory. The king of the Cannibal Islands never could have invented the printing press, because his mind contained neither the knowledge of the printing art nor the elements of a machine. No more can the clever but uneducated and untrained Yankee push out into the unknown in the complex fields of engineering and mechanics. He has not the storehouse from which he can bring " things new and old." These lofty heights are for our men of science. Second, here, in the absence of knowledge of the known, the old, lies the cause of endless reinvention — the endless procession of patent applications entering the Patent Office with high hopes, and destined to find an early grave in the Government cemetery of abandoned applications. More than 20,000 of these are interred annually.

Hence I would impress upon engineer and inventor a word of advice which is justified by the psychology of invention and the facts of experience: *Do not attempt to invent in a field the science and prior art of which are unknown to you.* And to this might be added a word of advice to the purchaser of patents or the employer of inventive skill: *Do not look for " grapes of thorns or figs of thistles."*

§ 18. The Twofold Character of Invention

To illustrate, let us take two most important inventions, wide apart in time and character.

The idea came to Elias Howe that he could put the eye of a needle adjacent to the point, carry a thread through a piece of cloth, slip a shuttle carrying a second thread through the loop carried down by the needle, and thus form a stitch.

During a series of laboratory experiments Edward G. Acheson discovered a substance he had produced which proved to be silica carbide — familiarly known as carborundum.

Suppose Howe and Acheson had done these things and no more: Would they have received patents? By no means. Before Howe could secure a patent on a sewing machine he had to devise the mechanical means which would operate his needle, which would operate his shuttle, which would feed the cloth along under the needle. If Acheson had done no more than to determine the character of the substance he found in his crucible without being able to state exactly the process by which it was produced and which would reproduce it, he would have had no patent eventuating in the great industry of making artificial abrasives. He developed the process so that he could make carborundum as a commercial product. Thus both went a distinct step farther than the mental act, and produced the "means whereby" their respective inventions might become useful.

But, it may be said, this is elemental and obvious. So it would seem; but so, as a matter of fact, it does *not* seem to a vast number of would-be inventors. The number of half-developed or mechanically impossible (alleged) inventions that come to any patent attorney is almost inconceivable — inconceivable that there should be such a percentage. Take this example as one of many: A man with a very limited knowledge of signal engineering comes to me with a cab-and-block signal system. He explains the apparatus and hastily traces the circuits, and wants a patent immediately. He is too obsessed with the value of his invention to view it critically; and after he leaves my office, I take a pad and diagram his circuits. Immediately I find that, in order to operate at all, every wheel on every locomotive, car, truck and hand car must be electrically insulated from its mate; so that if a railroad installed the system, it would be necessary to insulate the wheels of all of its rolling stock, and also all of the wheels of all of the cars and locomotives of all other railroads in the United States and Canada which might run over its tracks.

Nor is it the inventor alone who fails or falls. Take another leaf from experience: A half dozen men of capital and large experience had subscribed $10,000 to organize a company to exploit a wonderful invention in power generation. When they were about to draw their checks, one of them telephoned that he had "a suspicion," and asked me to investigate the invention. Here it is: Dig a circular pit and in its center place an electric generator of, say, 5000 horse-power capacity, the generator to have a vertical shaft. Attach to this shaft a sweep that will give a leverage of fifty to one. Build an endless track around the pit and place thereon a trolley car with a 100 horse-power motor, and hitch the sweep to this car. Then have a source of electric energy to start the car. As soon as the car starts, cut out this energy and take a like amount from the 5000 horse power generated in the pit to keep the car going. There you have a clean gain of 4900 horse power by perfectly simple arithmetic! Did such a thing ever happen? It certainly did; and, moreover, those men who were ready to put good money into it were not idiots, nor was the inventor a knave.

If these illustrations serve to reduce the number of inventors and investors who fail to think an invention through to the end — to the bitter end if need be — they will be pardonable.

But there is another matter which arises here and also in connection with the law of employer and employee elsewhere considered. Suppose that, when Elias Howe had conceived the idea of a sewing machine to the extent of making a needle with its eye adjacent to the point, and had then taken the needle to an employee and shown him how he could carry a thread through a piece of cloth, pass another thread through the loop, insert the needle at an adjacent point again and carry the under thread through the loop again, and then said, ' Now, I want you to put together a machine that will operate the needle, operate the shuttle, move the cloth along under the needle and devise the necessary tensions to hold the thread.' And suppose the employee does so and produces the Howe sewing machine. Who is the inventor and who can apply for a patent?

Quotations from two of the earlier leading cases in the patent law will clear the way somewhat. In Agawam v. Jordan, 74 U. S. 583; 19 L. Ed. 177, it was said:

When a person has discovered an improved principle in a machine, manufacture or composition of matter, and employs other persons to assist him in carrying out that principle, and they in the course of experiments arising from that employment make valuable discoveries ancillary to the plan and preconceived design of the employer, such suggested improvements are in general to be regarded as the property of the party who discovered the original improved principle, and may be embodied in his patent as a part of his invention.

And in the case of Union *v.* Vandeusen, 90 U. S. 530; 23 L. Ed. 128, the court said, in addition to quoting from Agawam *v.* Jordan, *supra.*

Persons employed, as much as employers, are entitled to their own independent inventions, and if the suggestions communicated constitute the whole substance of the improvement, the rule is otherwise, and the patent, if granted to the employer, is invalid, because the real invention or discovery belongs to the person who made the suggestion.

Hence, while it is true that invention is twofold and must be reduced to practice before it is a patentable invention, it is also true that the mere physical embodiment of an invention is not an inventive act per se.

But, suppose that, while this employee of Elias Howe was developing the sewing machine, he had conceived the idea that an adjustable feed that would vary the length of stitch would be useful, and had invented and attached it to Howe's machine. Who could patent and who would own this improvement? We shall consider the question of ownership in connection with the rights of employers and employees — where we shall find that it depends upon the nature of the employment. But regardless of who may own the patent on the improvement, it is perfectly clear that the invention is that of Howe's employee, and that he and he only can apply for a patent. The test always is, who originated the idea of means? That element of invention can never be delegated; the second element may. (See §§ 90, 91.)

§ 19. Reduction to Practice

We have seen that there is an abstract and a concrete side to patentable invention. But what constitutes reduction to practice? The statute (§ 4888) provides that

Before any inventor or discoverer shall receive a patent for his invention or discovery, he shall make application therefor, in writing, to the Commissioner of Patents, and shall file in the Patent Office a written description of the same, and of the manner and process of making, constructing, compounding, and using it, in such full, clear, concise, and exact terms as to enable any person skilled in the art or science to which it appertains, or with which it is most nearly connected, to make, construct, compound, and use the same; and in case of a machine, he shall explain the principle thereof and the best mode in which he has contemplated applying that principle, so as to distinguish it from other inventions; and he shall particularly point out and distinctly claim the part, improvement, or combination which he claims as his invention or discovery. The specification and claim shall be signed by the inventor and attested by two witnesses.

And § 4889 provides that a drawing shall be furnished whenever the case permits. Certainly, not until such a showing has been made, or that from which such a showing can be made, is an invention reduced to practice. But is such a paper showing reduction to practice according to the holdings of the courts? Here is one of the few raw edges of the patent law. It would be without purpose in this outline to go into the refinements of this question.[1] But three propositions may be laid down as settled:

1. Where a patent issues upon such a showing, it is sufficient, except in case of interference arising where priority is put in question.

2. Where a patent has been infringed, and the

[1] The opinion of Judge Holt in Automatic v. Pneumatic, 166 Fed. 288; 92 C. C. A. 206, is a treatise on this subject, and is excerpted fully in Mac. Pat. § 860.

specification and drawings clearly disclose the invention, such a showing is sufficient.

3: Where there is a contest over priority, conditions may arise where a paper showing is not reduction to practice, and later actual, physical reduction to practice may prevail.

§ 20. Invention and Mechanical Skill

The line between invention and mechanical skill is both shadowy and shifting. It is shadowy because we can never define invention exactly and because we can never define mechanical skill with much more success. It is shifting because engineering skill and mechanical efficiency are pushing the line farther and farther toward the unknown. What would have been invention fifty years ago is often mechanical skill to-day.[1] To revert again to the king of the Cannibal Islands,

[1] The case of Brown v. King, 107 Fed. 498; 46 C. C. A. 432, is of interest, because there the court recognized the fact that the line between invention and mechanical skill is a shifting one; and also because the court — by implication at least — made the mistake of applying one standard to an engineer and another to the untrained mechanic. This is manifestly erroneous; we cannot shift the line between invention and mechanical skill to make it a handicap to an inventor because he is trained and then move it the other way to make it a vantage to another inventor because he is untrained.

an improvement which he might make in pots for boiling missionaries might rise to the dignity of a new and useful invention — from his point of view; but the ordinary mechanic would make such a pot without a suspicion of doing more than mechanical service.

And here I desire to point out two lines of mistake frequently made by engineers. First, you may consider every advance or improvement which you make or have made as patentable improvement. This results in much foolish patenting. Scarecrow patents serve small purpose. Secondly, and on the other hand, too many engineers are prone to magnify their skill and minimize invention. They not infrequently allow small but important improvements to go unpatented. This is a self-evident failure to take advantage of a lawful and proper opportunity for your concern. But there is another and far more important reason for patenting all legitimate improvements, which is this: If you do not patent them, there is always the chance that another inventor will hit upon the same idea, patent it, and put you to the trouble and expense of defending in a suit for infringement. Hence, patent your legitimate improvements, not so much for the monopoly secured, but rather *as insurance against patent litigation.*

§ 21. Some General Rules

But how are you to know invention from mechanical skill? What are the earmarks of invention and what sort of a tag do you find on mechanical skill? How are you to know when something is worth patenting, or to know that a patent upon it is a waste of money? These are questions confronting engineers, and difficult ones to answer. There are some general rules which may be helpful.

1. Keep abreast of your art. This you may do by having a file of all American patents relating thereto. The Patent Office has all patents classified so that you may secure a file of these which directly concern you at comparatively small expense. Further, by making a small deposit in the Patent Office with your order, copies of all patents relating directly to your art will be sent you as issued.

2. Use your patent attorney to keep you out of trouble. Undoubtedly half of all patent litiga-

tion might be avoided by this means. It is far cheaper to pay your patent attorney consultation fees than to pay large bills for litigation.

3. Put an element of safety into your patent matters as you do in your construction. If some study will take your machine or process barely clear of the claims of a patent to another, more study will give a wider margin. In this way you will not only avoid danger of being mulcted by suit but also avoid probability of suit.

4. Establish a record system of all changes and improvements. This should contain prints or drawings and the names of persons able to testify to the facts. Such a record plays the same part as a system of bookkeeping, and will often enable you to establish priority of invention or use.

CHAPTER IV

WHAT IS PATENTABLE

§ 22. Introductory Statements

A FUNDAMENTAL cause of mind-fog on the subject of patents is failure to apprehend what is and what is not patentable. There is little reason for this, for, following explicitly the provision of the Constitution, the statute clearly defines what may be patented; and since no patent privilege exists at common law, nothing is patentable which falls outside these classes. The Constitution says that the grant may be made; and it says the grant shall be limited in three respects; namely, (1) " their respective discoveries "; hence, to the inventor and to no one else; (2) " for limited times "; hence, no perpetual monopoly; (3) " useful arts "; hence, every patent must possess utility.

Within these set boundaries Congress has defined the main divisions. The section already quoted (§ 4886) says: " Any person who has invented or discovered any new and useful art, machine, manufacture, or composition of matter, or any new and useful improvement thereof . . . ;" and in § 4929: "Any person who has invented any new, original and ornamental design for an article of manufacture . . . ;" and that is all. Nothing else is patentable in this country — an art, a machine, a manufacture, or a composition of matter, an improvement upon any one of these, a design. Clearly, there can be no "improvement" upon a design, any more than there could be an improvement upon a Rembrandt or a Turner. We shall now undertake to gain some definite knowledge of these five classes, but not in the order given in the statute; for it is easier to proceed from the simple to the complex. The order will be:

1. A Machine,
2. A Manufacture or Composition of Matter,
3. An Art,
4. An Improvement,
5. Designs.

In connection with these, illustrations will be used; and it is to be understood that these illustrations are for the purpose of illustration, and not for establishing fixed lines between the several classes.

§ 23. A Machine

The courts have written numerous definitions of a machine,[1] some of which are fairly satisfactory; but none is so good as the following by Robinson:[2]

It is an artificial organism, governed by a permanent artificial rule of action, receiving crude mechanical force from the motive power, and multiplying or transforming it according to the mode established by the rule.

We shall do better, however, in illustrating rather than defining. Let us take the Selden patent which was the subject of a famous litigation, and to which we shall have occasion to refer in other connections. The annexed are the principal drawings of the patent.

The first and main claim of this patent reads:

1. The combination with a road locomotive, provided with suitable running gear including a propelling wheel and steering mechanism, of a liquid hydrocarbon gas-engine of the compression type, comprising one or more power cylinders, a suitable liquid fuel receptacle, a power shaft connected with and arranged to run faster than the propelling wheel, an intermediate clutch or dis-

---

[1] Mac. Pat. § 768.   [2] Rob. Pat. § 173.

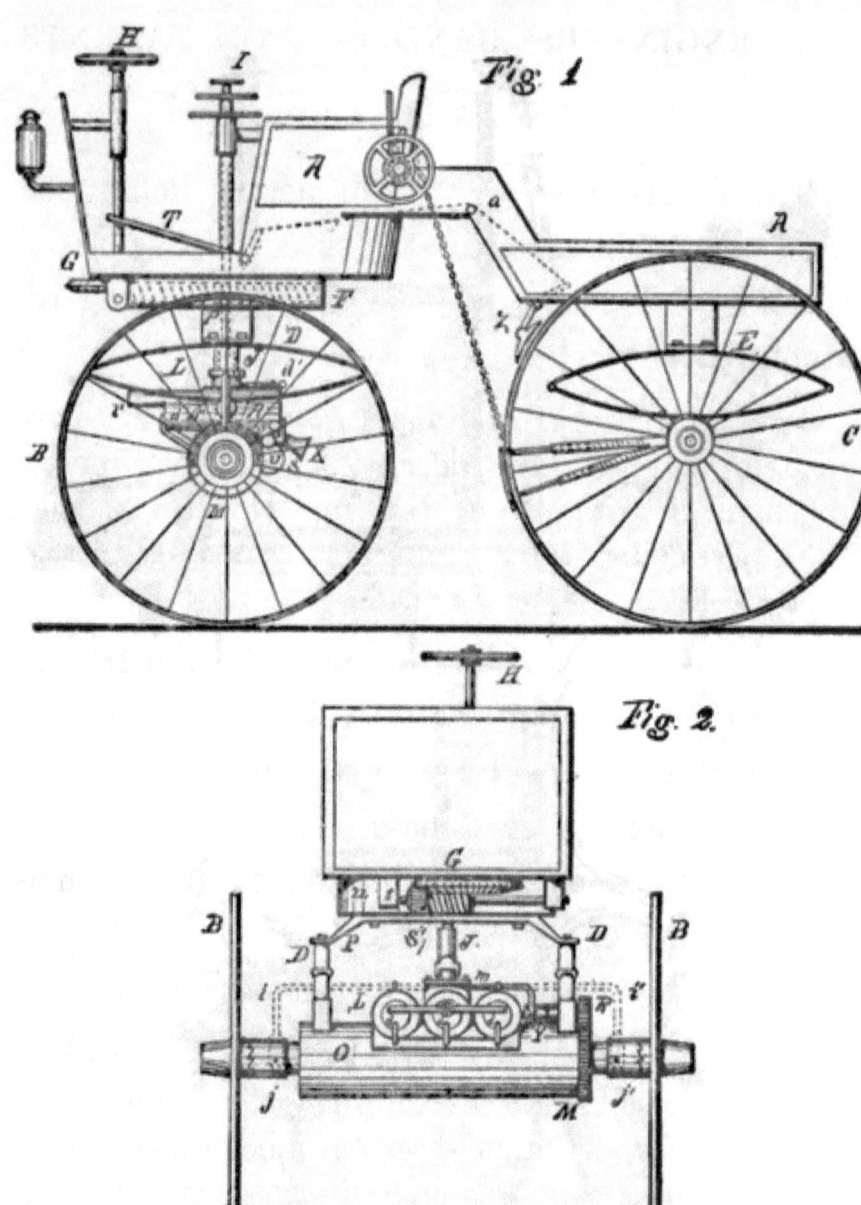

SELDEN ROAD ENGINE

CALIFORNIA

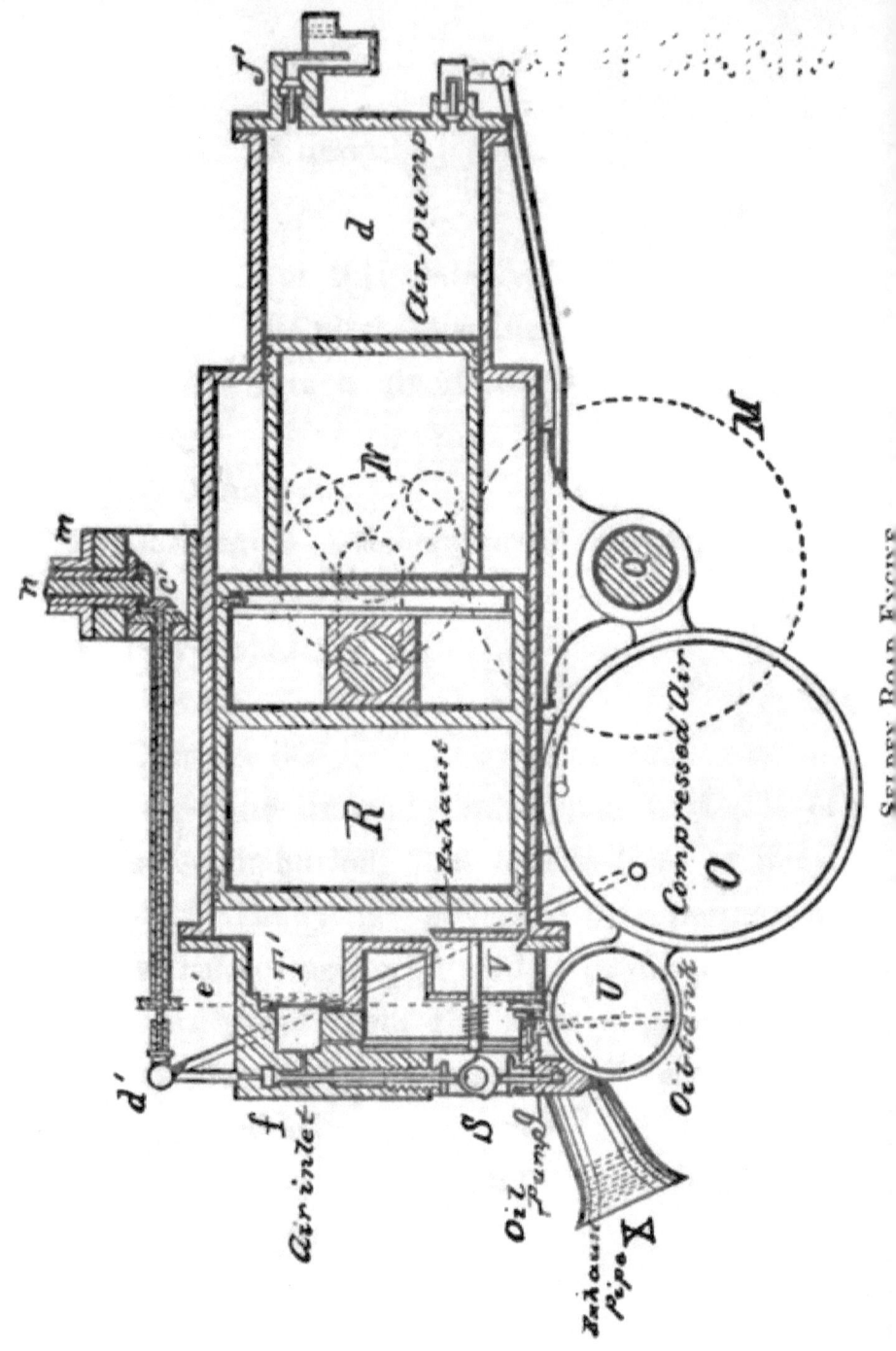

SELDEN ROAD ENGINE

connecting device and a suitable carriage body adapted to the conveyance of persons or goods, substantially as described.

An analysis of this claim will show that it is made up of definitely specified elements which coact to perform a given function. These elements are:

1. Running gear,
2. Gas-engine of the compression type,
3. Fuel receptacle,
4. Power shaft,
5. Clutch,
6. Carriage body.

We have no difficulty in saying, in terms of Robinson's definition, that this is " an artificial organism "; that it is " governed by a permanent artificial rule of action "; that it receives " crude mechanical force from the motive power "; or that it multiplies or transforms it " according to the mode established by the rule."

But it is also to be noted that we have here more than a single machine. The gas-engine, by itself, is a machine; the steering apparatus, by itself, is a machine. Very many so-called machines are combinations of several machines — for example, the automobile of which this Selden machine is a prototype is made up of a large number of machines. It therefore follows that mere complexity is not the test.

Yet it is by no means easy to discriminate sharply at all times between a machine and an article of manufacture. Compare three common devices — an ordinary pen, a fountain pen, and a writing machine. It is evident that an ordinary pen is not a machine, any more than a paint brush. The rule of action does not reside in the pen; you must not only apply force, but you must direct that force; you must dip the pen in ink and form the characters by the mechanism of your hand in order to make it write. With the writing machine you simply apply force. The law of the machine is that, when you strike a certain character, a corresponding character will be printed on paper. You do not have to form the character. Moreover, there is another machine within this machine which moves the carriage step by step; another that moves the ribbon; another that shifts the paper; another that rings the bell when the end of a line is reached. No doubt this is a machine which is a combination of several machines. But how about the fountain pen? As a pen, it is simply a pen — a tool, an implement, an article of manufacture. But it does not have to be dipped in ink. It contains mechanism whereby, when pressure is applied, ink is carried down to the pen. That is the law of the device; you do not have to give thought or attention to it; it is the law of the machine that ink shall flow to the pen when you apply pressure to the point. It is, therefore, a machine — not a machine for writing, but a machine for supplying ink to a pen.

While we shall consider the difference between a true combination and an aggregation elsewhere, it is well to note here that mere aggregation does not constitute a machine. For example, suppose you attach to your automobile a device for lighting your lamps, whereby you can turn on the gas and light it at the burners from your seat in the car. This may be a very handy attachment, and in itself may be patentable; but it and the automobile do not coact to form a machine. A clip attached to my fountain pen to hold it in my pocket is a very desirable device, and may be patentable; but it in no wise relates to or modifies the fountain pen as a machine for supplying ink to a pen.

And one of the tests of a machine is whether, when some element fails of its function, the machine stops. Removal of the clip does not stop my fountain pen from acting. Removal of your lamp-lighting device does not stop your automobile; but suppose your clutch fails to work. There is one test. The fact that your machine stops — fails to obey its rule of action — is evidence that it has ceased to be a machine, and has, for the time being, become a mere aggregation.

§ 24. A Manufacture or Composition of Matter

Dr. Robinson defines a manufacture as "an instrument created by the exercise of mechanical forces and designed for the production of mechanical effects, but not capable, when set in motion, of attaining by its own operation to any determined result."[1] He defines a composition of matter as "an instrument formed by the intermixture of two or more ingredients, and possessing properties which belong to none of these in-

[1] Rob. Pat. § 182.

gredients in their separate state."[1] The Supreme Court has said of a manufacture: "The Patent Office fully comprehends the rule that new articles of commerce are not patentable as new manufactures, unless it appears in the given case that the production of the new articles involved the exercise of invention or discovery beyond what was necessary to construct the apparatus for its manufacture or production."[2] And that court said, in speaking of an artificial dyestuff:[3] "While a new process for producing it was patentable, the product itself could not be patented, even though it was a product made artificially for the first time, in contradistinction to being eliminated from the madder root. Calling it artificial alizarine did not make it a new composition of matter and patentable as such, by reason of its having been prepared artificially for the first time from anthracine, if it was set forth as alizarine, a well-known substance."

Thus we have the definitions of the textbook writer and the limitations set by the Supreme

---

[1] Rob. Pat. § 192.
[2] Milligan v. Upton, 97 U. S. 3; 24 L. Ed. 985.
[3] Cochrane v. Badische, 111 U. S. 293; 28 L. Ed. 455.

Court upon a patentable article of manufacture and a composition of matter. It is all too easy to pick flaws in a definition or find a seeming exception to a rule of law. For example, suppose soap to be a newly discovered composition: It clearly falls within the definition of a composition of matter, but would it be nonpatentable in view of the fact that soap bark has existed always? Would it thus fall under the rule of the Dyestuff Case? I think not. Then suppose we add sand to it and make it sand soap: at once it is taken out from the class of compositions of matter as defined by Robinson, because it does not possess " properties which belong to none of those ingredients." It would then be an article of manufacture, seemingly. Hence it must be borne in mind that definition and delimitation can be, in the nature of things, no more than relative.

Let us now take two illustrations which stand at the two ends of this complex class. Annexed are the drawings of the patent in the famous Collar Button Case.[1]

The claim of this patent reads:

---

[1] Krementz *v.* Cottle, 148 U. S. 556; 37 L. Ed. 558; 13 S. Ct. 719.

Fig. 1

Fig. 2

Fig. 3

Fig. 4

Fig. 5

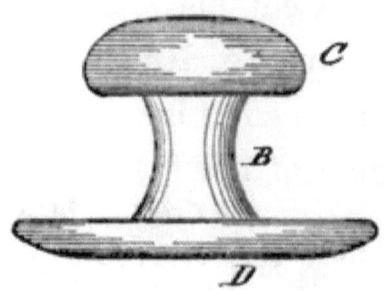

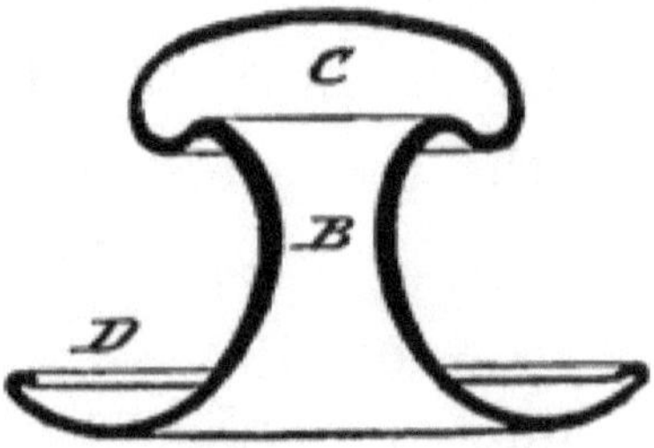

Collar Button Patent

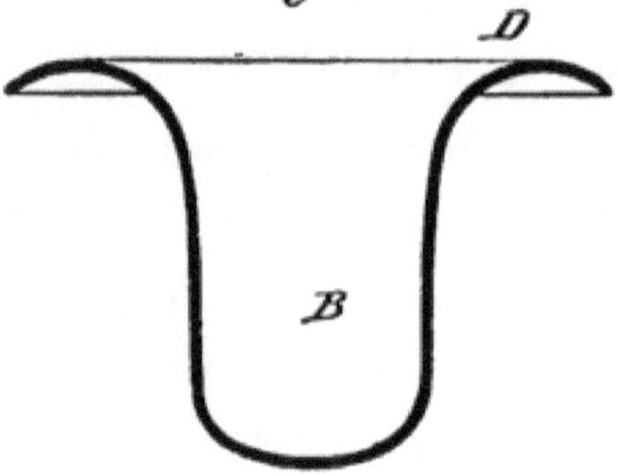

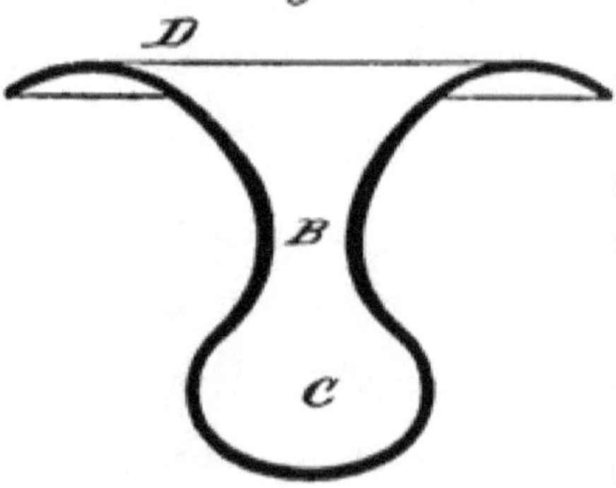

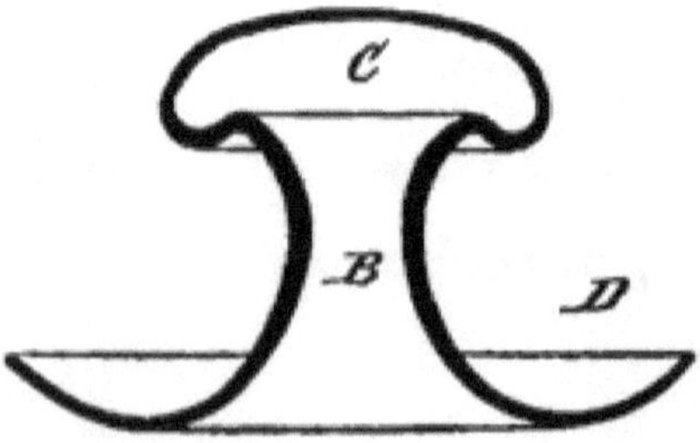

A collar or sleeve button having a hollow bead and stem, the said head, stem and the base plate or back of said button being shaped and made of a single continuous piece of sheet metal, substantially as herein shown and described.

This patent was held valid for an article of manufacture. At the other end of the line stands the Phenacetine Patent.[1] The claim of this patent reads:

The product herein described which has the following characteristics: It crystallizes in white leaves, melting at 135° centigrade; not coloring on addition of acids or alkalies; is little soluble in cold water; more so in hot water; easily soluble in alcohol, ether, chloroform, or benzole; is without taste; and has the general composition $C_{10}H_{13}O_2N$.

This patent was held valid after strenuous contest, and is clearly a composition of matter. Between these clear-cut examples under the two definitions lie an enormous number of things that are articles of manufacture or compositions of matter, so shading together that it is often difficult to say to which part of this class they belong. These two illustrations serve to mark the out-boundaries.

[1] Maurer *v.* Dickerson, 113 Fed. 870; 51 C. C. A. 494.

True patentable articles of manufacture are numerous, while true patentable compositions of matter are few. Most composition patents, if put to test, fall under the rule of the Dyestuff Case above noted. For example, it is claimed that a process for producing artificial rubber has been discovered. Undoubtedly the process is patentable, but would artificial rubber as a composition of matter be patentable? Certainly not if it be true synthetic rubber.

And here a word to the engineer and the manufacturer is in place. A patentee or a promoter will come to you with, let us say, a new kind of artificial stone. He has a patent upon his machine and another upon his process, and his trump card is a patent upon the stone as a composition of matter. His machine patent probably has valid but limited claims; his process patent is more doubtful and requires careful scrutiny; his composition patent is probably invalid. Not until the searchlight of expert examination has been applied and not until the acid test of court rulings has failed, should such a patent be accepted.

§ 25. An Art or Process

The statute mentions neither a process nor a method as one of the classes of patentable invention. It uses the broad, comprehensive term "art." The Supreme Court, in the Telephone Cases,[1] defined this term by illustration, saying:

In this art — or, what is the same thing under the patent law, this process, this way of transmitting speech — electricity, one of the forces of nature, is employed; but electricity, left to itself, will not do what is wanted. The art consists in so controlling the force as to make it accomplish the purpose. . . . Bell discovered that it could be done by gradually changing the intensity of a continuous electric current, so as to make it correspond exactly to the change in density of the air caused by the sound of the voice. This was his art.

The thing which Bell patented was a machine — a telephone; but that patent contained what amounted to an art or process claim. This, as we shall see later, was proper. The process of making nitroglycerine was a new and useful "art," and patentable; and the article itself, as a manufacture or composition of matter, was patentable.

[1] 126 U. S. 1; 31 L. Ed. 863; 8 S. Ct. 778.

Aërial navigation is a new and useful "art"; but it is self-evident that no one will be granted a patent on the art of flying. Many patents are being issued on machines used in the art. Nor does it help matters to say that the meaning of the statute is the "mechanical arts," for so defined, in spite of the qualifications of novelty and utility imposed by the statute, it is still too broad; for it would include many things which are mere mechanical skill. We have all seen persons possessed of some remarkable mechanical art, such as turning an almost perfect sphere, or giving a tool a remarkably fine temper, or dyeing an article with remarkable exactness. These are mechanical arts — arts of individuals — but they are not, per se, patentable.

And yet, the use of the term in the statute has been a most desirable one, since its very vagueness has produced a resiliency in the otherwise hard-and-fast terms of the statute, and has enabled the Patent Office and the courts to reward those pioneers whose basic discoveries have often been too large, too simple, too generic to be limited to a specific machine or the specific steps of a given process. It would not be far from the truth to say

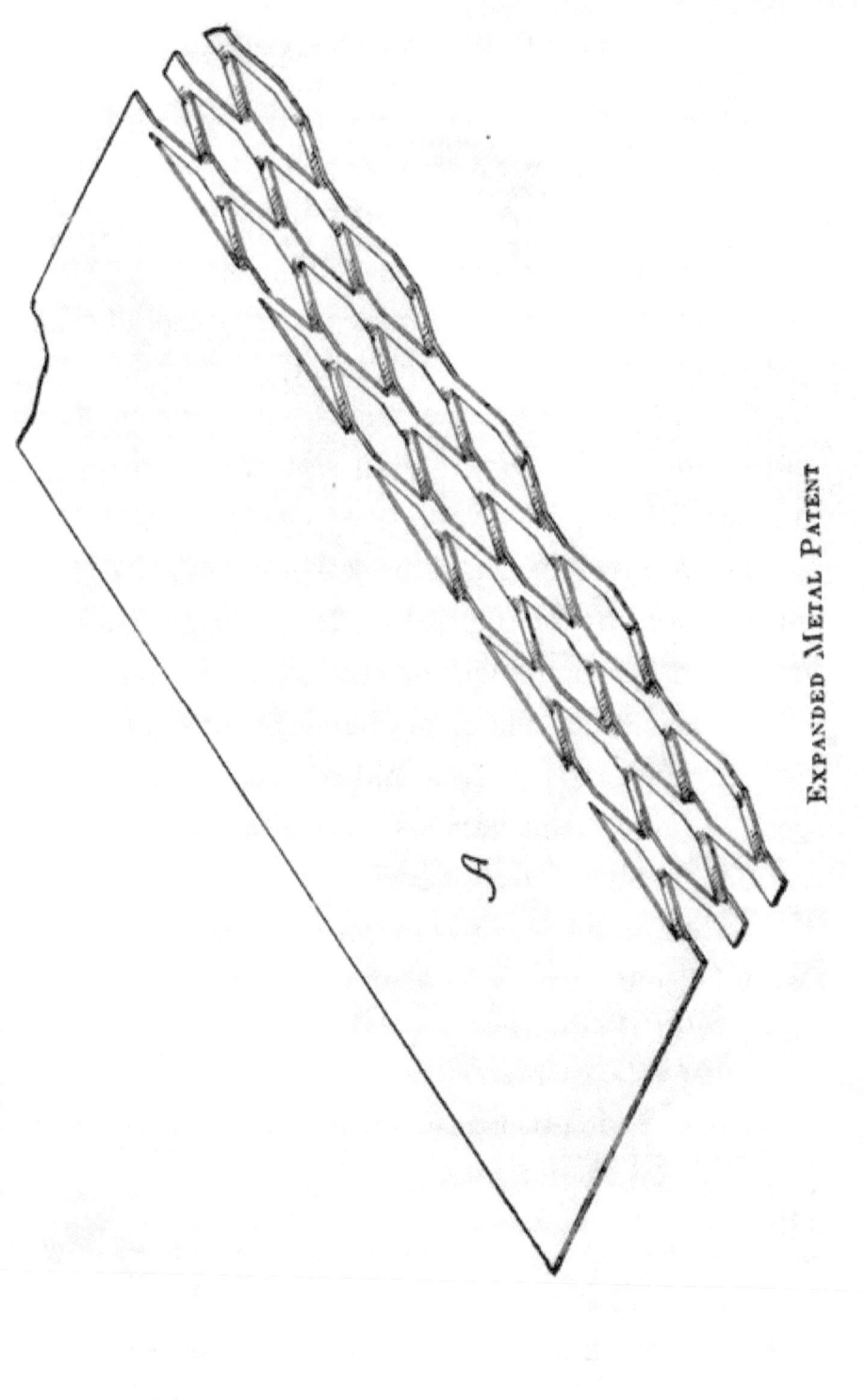

Expanded Metal Patent

that the term "art," as used in the statute, has opened the way for the courts to build up the doctrine of equivalents and establish that aristocracy among inventors known as "Pioneers."

The practice of a patentable art may include the use of a machine; but the machine may be old. The result of the process may be either a new or old product. It may produce a composition of matter either new or old.

That a novel chemical process is patentable, the courts have never doubted. It is only when the process is mechanical, producing some physical effect other than chemical change, that conflict of opinion has arisen. It would serve no useful purpose to follow the various rulings and change of opinion,[1] since the Expanded Metal Case [2] sets the question at rest. That case is of special interest now and later. The annexed cut shows the product of this patent.

---

[1] The rule as to patentability of mechanical processes may be traced in reading McClurg v. Kingsland, 1 How. 202; 11 L. Ed. 102; Tilghman v. Proctor, 102 U. S. 707; 26 L. Ed. 279; Telephone Cases, *supra* Risdon v. Medart, 158 U. S. 68; 39 L. Ed. 899; 15 S. Ct. 745; Westinghouse v. Boyden, 170 U. S. 537; 42 L. Ed. 1136; 18 S. Ct. 707; Carnegie v. Cambria, 185 U. S. 403; 46 L. Ed. 968; 22 S. Ct. 698.

[2] Expanded v. Bradford, 214 U. S. 366; 53 L. Ed. 1034.

The claim of the patent reads:

The herein described method of making open or reticulated metal work, which consists in simultaneously slitting and bending portions of a plate of sheet metal in such manner as to stretch or elongate the bars connecting the slit portions and body of the sheet or plate, and then simultaneously slitting and bending in places alternate to the first mentioned portions, thus producing the finished expanded sheet metal of the same length as that of the original sheet or plate, substantially as described.

But wherein lies the process? It will be seen from an examination of the patent that it consists in slitting and stretching down the metal at right angles to the plane of the sheet. This slitting, stretching, and distorting it beyond the elastic limit, so that it takes a permanent set and remains rigid and flat. To this extent the character of the metal was modified by the process. Compare this with the old method shown in the annexed cut from the Golding and Durkee patent.

Here the slits are cut and the metal stretched out in plane with the sheet; with the result that a buckling, stretchable, irregular piece is formed.

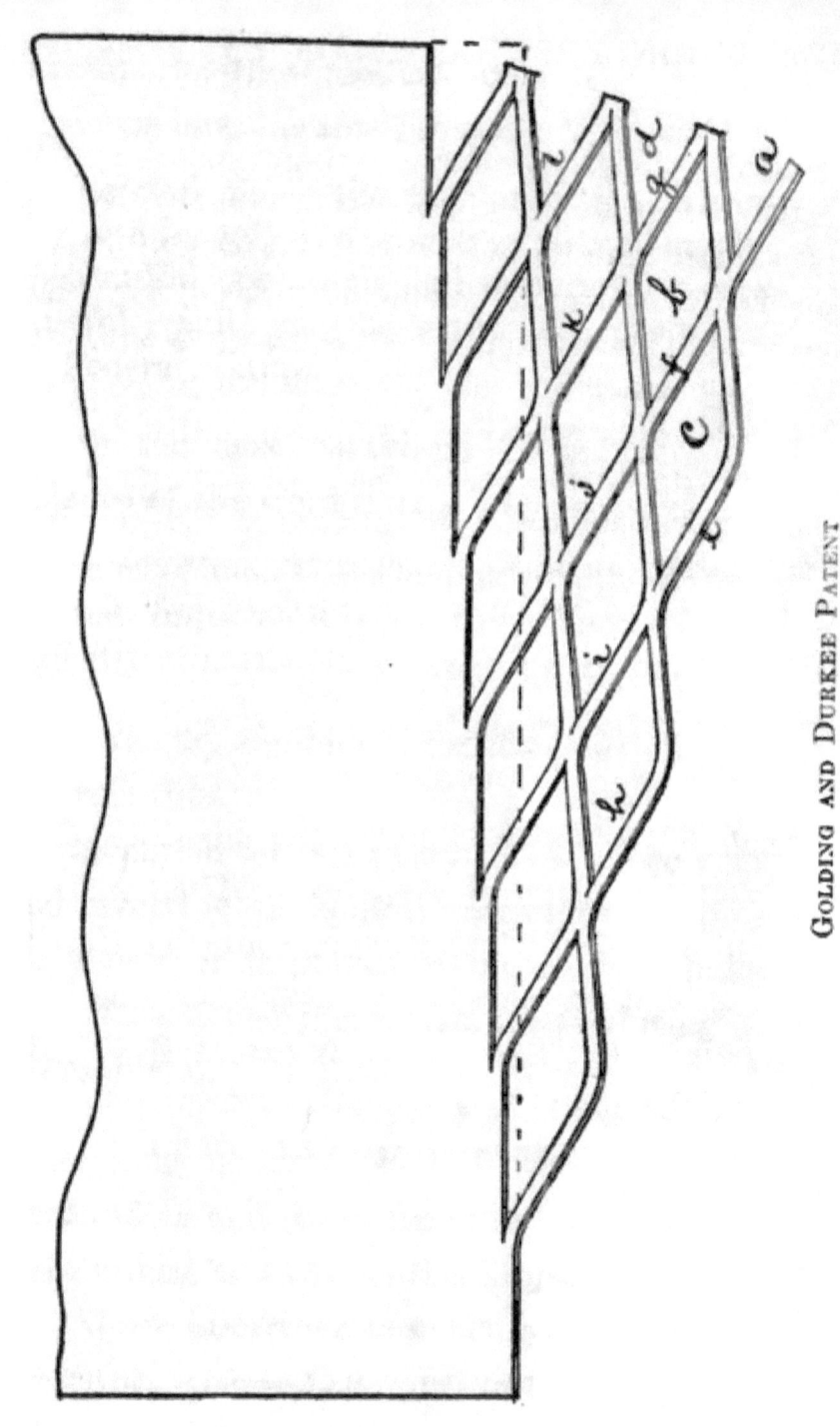

Golding and Durkee Patent

After comparing these methods and after reviewing the previous law, Justice Day said:

We therefore reach the conclusion that an invention or discovery of a process or method involving mechanical operations and performing a new and useful result, *may* be within the protection of the Federal statute.

And in the next paragraph he indicates the significance of the word " may " by saying:

We are of opinion that Golding's method was a substantial improvement of this character, independently of particular means for performing it.

Hence we may combine these statements into a general rule thus:

The invention or discovery of a process or method involving mechanical operations and producing a new or improved result may, if independent of particular mechanism for producing it, be patentable.

§ 26. An Improvement

The standing and character of an improvement was established as early as the Morse Telegraph Case.[1] Morse undertook to so claim and monopo-

---
[1] O'Reilly *v.* Morse, 15 How. 62; 14 L. Ed. 601.

lize all possible methods of transmitting information by the use of an electric current that it would have been impossible to make and use any improvement during the life of his patent. This the Supreme Court would not permit, and held that Morse or any one else might improve upon his telegraph apparatus and patent it.

But while you may improve upon a machine, manufacture, process, or art and patent your improvement, you will have no right arising thereby to use the thing improved upon if it is patented and the patent in force. Nor will the original patentee have any right to your invention, merely because he holds the dominant patent.[1]

§ 27. A Design

No better definition of a design can be found than that of Judge Grosscup:[2]

Design, in the view of the patent law, is that characteristic of a physical substance which, by means of lines, images, configuration, and the like, taken as a whole, makes an impression, through the eye, upon the mind of the observer. The

---

[1] Mac. Pat. §§ 436, 506, 507.
[2] Pelouze v. American, 102 Fed. 916; 43 C. C. A. 52.

essence of a design resides not in the elements individually, nor in the method of arrangement, but in the tout ensemble — in that indefinable whole that awakens some sensation in the observer's mind. Impressions thus imparted may be complex or simple; in one a mingled impression of gracefulness and strength, in another the impression of strength alone. But whatever the impression, there is attached in the mind of the observer to the object observed a sense of uniqueness and character.

This is in perfect accord with the present-day rulings.[1] A patentable design does not come from the same corner of the brain as a machine or a process, or even an article of manufacture. It is distinctly the product of the exercise of the æsthetic powers. It is a unit; you cannot dissect it or divide it into component elements, as you can a machine; and the test of a design invention is whether it appeals to the eye of a competent observer as an æsthetic creation. But do not misapprehend that statement. You have seen, at Christmas time, for example, a toy bank displayed in shop windows, consisting of a cast-iron negro

[1] Smith v. Whitman, 148 U. S. 674; 37 L. Ed. 606; 13 S. Ct. 768; Williams v. Kemmerer, 145 Fed. 928; 76 C. C. A. 466.

with a grin of sufficient expansion to receive a coin. You will not find this design in a museum of fine arts, but it is a good patentable design. The question is not always beauty of design, but rather individuality which distinguishes it from all other designs through the æsthetic sense.

One word of caution at this point. You will find cases holding that the test of design novelty or infringement is whether an ordinary person would mistake the one for the other. This is the familiar rule as to trade-marks; but attempt to apply it to designs is far from safe. A trade-mark upon an article gives no value, per se, to the article — adds no whit to its desirability. It simply identifies the article, and helps the purchaser to pick out the particular brand or kind he wants. A design imposes a value upon the article; a trade-mark merely identifies it. Hence it should be evident that the mental act which enables the ordinary workman to identify his favorite brand of plug tobacco when he sees a tin star on it, is quite another thing from that which persuades you to purchase a handsome design in silverware; and to say they are one and the same test is wide of the mark.

§ 28. Summary of these Classes

We identify a machine by finding in it the law of its being — the implanted law of the inventor. We find the one-piece collar button a patentable article of manufacture; and we at once say such a new chemical compound as phenacetine is a patentable composition of matter. Between these we find a host of articles and compounds which belong within this broad class, but which are not always distinguishable as articles of manufacture or as compositions of matter. We identify a process as a recipe for taking certain steps which result in a new product, or an old product produced in a different or more advantageous manner. We find a mechanical process patentable, provided the process is independent of any special means or mechanism for carrying it on. Improvements upon any of these classes are distinctly within the statute; but improver and improved are alike limited to their own fields of invention. A design, upon which there can be no improvement, is the product of true inventive genius, but consists in an entirety which appeals to another faculty of the mind — the æsthetic sense.

Nothing but that which falls within one of these classes is patentable.

§ 29. Things not Patentable

While we cannot define invention, and while we should have trouble of we undertook to catalogue all things patentable and all things not patentable, we may classify certain things which are not patentable by applying the two principles of the inventive act — the mental process and the physical process — and also applying the strict limitations of the statute. In each of the following instances it will be found that either one or the other of the factors of invention is wanting, or that the thing clearly falls outside the patentable classes specified by the statute.

¶ 1. *Mental Conception*

As Justice Lurton once said:[1]

The mere existence of an intellectual notion that a certain thing could be done, and, if done, might be of practical utility, does not furnish a basis for a patent, or estop others from developing the same idea.

[1] Standard *v.* Peters, 77 Fed. 630; 23 C. C. A. 367.

This is obvious; the second factor of the inventive act has not entered in; it has not become a concretion; in fact, in most such cases, we find, instead of a true mental conception, a mental fog. But let us make no mistake here. The judge writing the opinion in the Expanded Metal Case when before the circuit court of appeals,[1] said:

As we regard the application (that of the process of slitting and bending the metal) it was the announcement of no more than a happy thought.

And the court held the patent invalid. But the Supreme Court thought otherwise.[2] Why? Because the inventor not only had a "happy thought," but he reduced it to practice and laid the foundation for a large industry. Invention is not measurable in terms of time or effort. It may come like a flash, or be the result of long study. It may be reduced to practice by the simplest means, or it may take years to do it.

¶ 2. *A Force of Nature*

Morse sought to monopolize the electric current as a force of nature for transmitting informa-

---

[1] Bradford *v.* Expanded, 146 Fed. 984; 77 C. C. A. 230.
[2] Expanded *v.* Bradford, 214 U. S. 366; 53 L. Ed. 1034; 29 S. Ct. 652.

tion. This he was not permitted to do.¹ No more could Madame Curie patent polonium; but she could patent a device for putting it to some practical use.

¶ 3. *Scientific Principles*

Justice McLean said in the Lead Pipe Case:[2]

> A principle, in the abstract, is a fundamental truth; an original cause; a motive; these cannot be patented, and no one can claim in either of them an exclusive right.

This case is of special interest upon this and the next following subjects, and may be explained briefly. It had been discovered that lead and similar metals and alloys having a low fusing point could, by the application of a degree of heat less than sufficient to melt them and by the application of high pressure, be made to flow and to unite, so as to form lead pipe, traps, and the like. It was the discovery of a scientific principle and a property of matter. Neither was patentable, but the machine employing this principle and taking advantage of this property of matter was patentable;

---

[1] O'Reilly v. Morse, 15 How. 62; 14 L. Ed. 601.
[2] LeRoy v. Tatham, 14 How. 156; 14 L. Ed. 367.

and under the present rule of patentability of a mechanical process, the process also might have been patentable. But while a force of nature may not be patented, one may state in scientific terminology the method of practicing a given art without violation of this rule.[1]

¶ 4. *Property of Matter*

As we have seen from the Lead Pipe Case, *supra*, a property of matter is not patentable; but the practical application of it may be. The Incandescent Lamp Case [2] set the limit properly. The Sawyer-Man Patent, there in litigation, undertook to cover broadly every known fiber that could make a lamp filament — in other words, to cover the property of matter found in vegetable fiber that made a lamp filament possible. Of course, such a claim could not stand.

¶ 5. *Result or Function*

A patent is not good for an effect, or result of a given process, as that would prohibit all other persons from making the same by any means whatsoever.[3]

---

[1] Westinghouse *v.* Saranac, 113 Fed. 884; 51 C. C. A. 514.
[2] 159 U. S. 465; 40 L. Ed. 221; 16 S. Ct. 75.
[3] LeRoy *v.* Tatham, 14 How. 156; 14 L. Ed. 367.

It is for the discovery or invention of some practical method or means of producing a beneficial result or effect that a patent is granted, and not for the result or effect itself.[1]

The one exception — but, after all, not an exception — is where the method or process results in a new composition of matter which would be patentable regardless of the method or process of producing it. For example, the process of making phenacetine might have been patentable, and phenacetine as a composition of matter was patentable, not because it was a result or function of a novel process, but because it chanced to be a novel composition of matter.

¶ 6. *Aggregation*

The simplest illustration is the Rubber Tip Pencil Case.[2] This patent covered the ordinary lead pencil which has a rubber eraser inserted in one end in line with the lead, which may be exposed by sharpening, the same as the lead. The Supreme Court held this to be aggregation, because neither element modified the function of the other — one end up it was a pencil, the other end up it

---

[1] Corning *v.* Burden, 15 How. 252; 14 L. Ed. 683.
[2] Reckendorfer *v.* Faber, 92 U. S. 347; 23 L. Ed. 719.

was an eraser. The best illustration is the Elevator Case.[1] Here the patent covered a grain elevator having the ordinary leg for entering the hatch of a vessel, and a second leg mounted upon a truck which traveled on rails on the wharf beside the elevator, so that the movable leg could be brought to the right position to enter a second hatch of the same vessel. It was a most useful device and went into general use; but it was not patentable, because neither leg and its mechanism in any way modified the action of the other; it was valuable, but none the less an aggregation.

¶ 7. *Duplication*

This is obvious if it is pure duplication.[2]

¶ 8. *Simplification*

While it is, perhaps, true that sometimes the mere simplification of mechanism by omitting parts may amount to patentable invention, yet this is only under exceptional circumstances.[3]

The "exceptional circumstances" are those

---

[1] Dunbar *v.* Eastern, 81 Fed. 201; 26 C. C. A. 330.
[2] Topliff *v.* Topliff, 145 U. S. 156; 36 L. Ed. 568; 12 S. Ct. 825.
[3] U. S. Peg Wood *v.* Sturtevant, 125 Fed. 378; 60 C. C. A. 244.

which, by omission or simplification, make a change in the combination. Whenever you have simplification held patentable, you will find something more than that; you will find either a change of combination, constituents, or steps which render it a different thing.

¶ 9. *Double Use or Analogous Use*

The law on this subject is summed up by Justice Brown in the Clay Disintegrator Case,[1] in which the patent was held valid because the eight prior devices were held not to be analogous use. It is worth while to quote this case somewhat fully:

Doubtless a patentee is entitled to every use of which his invention is susceptible, whether such use be known or unknown to him; but the person who has taken his device and, by improvements thereon, has adapted it to a different industry, may also draw to himself the quality of inventor. If, for instance, a person were to take a coffee mill and patent it as a mill for grinding spices, the double use would be too manifest. So, too, this court has denied invention to one who applied the principle of an ice cream freezer to the preservation of fish (Brown *v.* Piper, 91 U. S. 37); to

---

[1] Potts *v.* Creager, 155 U. S. 597; 39 L. Ed. 275; 15 S. Ct. 194.

another who changed the proportions of a refrigerator in such manner as to utilize the descending instead of the ascending current of cold air (Roberts v. Ryer, 91 U. S. 150); to another who employed an old and well-known method of attaching car-trucks to the forward truck of a locomotive engine (Pennsylvania v. Locomotive, 110 U. S. 490); and to still another who placed a dredging screw at the stem instead of the stern of a steamboat (Atlantic v. Brady, 107 U. S. 192). In Tucker v. Spalding, 80 U. S. 453, the patent covered the use of movable teeth in saws and saw plates. A prior patent exhibited cutters of the same general form as the saw teeth of the other patent, attached to a circular disk, and removable as in the other, the purpose of which was for the cutting of tongues and grooves, mortices, etc. The court held that if what it actually did was in the nature of sawing, and its structure and action suggested to the mind of an ordinary skilled mechanic this double use to which it could be adapted without material change, then such adaptation to a new use was not invention, and was not patentable.

Upon the other hand, we have recently upheld a patent to one who took a torsional spring, such as had been previously used in clocks, doors, and other articles of domestic furniture, and applied it to telegraph instruments, the application being shown to be wholly new. Western v. LaRue, 139 U. S. 601.

Clearly, then, a double use is not patentable, and equally clearly an analogous use is not patentable. But the difficulty arises in determining in a specific instance whether the use is or is not analogous. Here is where "mortal mind" determines; and I know of nothing more fallible or relative than "mortal mind."

¶ 10. *Transposition of Parts*

This evidently is not invention.[1] But there are cases where what appears, at first sight, to be mere transposition of parts turns out to be the creation of a new combination, and as such is patentable.[2]

¶ 11. *Immoral Object*

It is clear that an invention which would be detrimental to public morals or human welfare would lack one of the requisites of the statute. It might be new and most ingenious, but it would not be useful; and the statute says "new and useful."[3]

§ 30. Things Generally Nonpatentable

These are acts or things generally nonpatentable

---

[1] Penfield v. Chambers, 92 Fed. 630; 34 C. C. A. 579.
[2] International v. Kellogg, 171 Fed. 651; 96 C. C. A. 395.
[3] See Mac. Pat. § 645.

but which may, under certain conditions, involve patentable invention.

Here is one of the battle grounds of invention. It is too conflicting, too technical, for exhaustive treatment. But a few illustrative cases will serve to show the situation. There is an old saying that judicial discretion varies directly with the length of the chancellor's boot. The saying does not say whether the variation is increase or decrease, but like most old saws it contains an element of truth. Pilate had the right to ask "What is truth?" If he were to read the cases bearing upon this topic, he might well ask "What is invention?" For we are now on the border line between invention and mechanical skill, the line always shifting between that which we call invention but cannot definitely define, and that which we call mechanical skill which we cannot delimit.

It is here that the engineer as a man of science, as an expert, plays a large part and performs high service; for, while the question of invention or noninvention must ultimately be settled by the court or the jury, the court or the jury must have the facts as they stand related to the prior art and illumined by scientific analysis. It used to be common for the English chancellor to call to the bench beside him an engineer of great learning to advise him in the decision of a difficult patent cause. Unfortunately, such practice has not prevailed in this country; but it is true, none the less, that our courts place much reliance upon the opinions of engineers testifying as experts, as we shall see later.

Turning to those things on the border line, the first is:

¶ 1. *Adaptation*

The old Door Knob Case,[1] the patent for which was issued over the signature of Daniel Webster as Secretary of State, is typical. The patent covered the ordinary "china" door knob, in which the metallic shank is held in place in the porcelain or clay knob by lead poured into the cavity in the knob and about the end of the shank. To secure one object to another by means of a lead filling about a bolt, or an eye, or a shank, was well known; but this patent claimed the adaptation of this old method of securing a shank in a porcelain or clay knob. The court held the patent bad as being mere adaptation. But not all cases are as

---

[1] Hotchkiss *v.* Greenwood, 11 How. 248; 13 L. Ed. 683.

clear as this;[1] and the Selden Case[2] is one where both courts and experts disagreed as to whether the adaptation of the Brayton engine amounted to invention.

On the other hand, take the case where Edison changed the leading-in wires of the incandescent lamp,[3] where he merely adapted the metals to conditions involved. This was a thing not apparent, a thing desired and sought after, and was true invention.

¶ 2. *Carrying Forward*

But a mere carrying forward, or a new or more extended application of the original thought, a change only in form, proportion or degree, the substitution of equivalents, doing substantially the same thing in substantially the same way by substantially the same means with better results, is not such invention as will sustain a patent.[4]

Here, again, the Selden Case is a good example. As the circuit court saw it, Selden did carry forward the old gas-engine sufficiently to amount to invention. The appellate court thought other-

---

[1] Mac. Pat. §§ 591–593.
[2] Columbia *v.* Duerr, 184 Fed. 893; 107 C. C. A. 215.
[3] Edison *v.* Novelty, 167 Fed. 977; 93 C. C. A. 387.
[4] Smith *v.* Nichols, 88 U. S. 112; 22 L. Ed. 566.

wise. There is little doubt in my mind that, if Selden, starting with the improvements shown in his patent, had gone forward and produced a successful automobile, the patent would have been held valid.

¶ 3. *Change of Form*

The cases holding mere change of form without change of function to be unpatentable are numerous.[1] But from Winans v. Denmead [2] down to the Rubber Tire Case,[3] it has always been held that, where form is of the essence of the invention, patentability may exist.

¶ 4. *Substitution*

As we shall see when we come to the subject of equivalents (§ 62), the substitution of an element which is an equivalent does not avoid infringement, and so could not involve invention. And it is evident that the mere substitution of one material for another is not invention.[4]

But it was no mere act of substitution for Edison

---

[1] Mac. Pat. §§ 600–602, 655.
[2] Winans v. Denmead, 15 How. 330; 14 L. Ed. 717.
[3] Diamond Rubber v. Consolidated, 220 U. S. 428; 55 L. Ed. 527; 31 S. Ct. 444.
[4] Mac. Pat. § 696.

to discover, after making tests of some 40,000 different kinds of material, the one species of bamboo which turned the old platinum lamp into the commercial lamp of to-day.[1]

¶ 5. *Systems and Arrangements*

A system of bookkeeping is not patentable; a cash-register system is not patentable; a system of freight billing is not patentable; a system for handling passengers at a railway terminal is not patentable; nor is a telephone system patentable.[2] But the appellate court decided against me when I urged that a block-signal system for railways was unpatentable.[3] Why? Because the court found that one unit of the system modified the action of the next unit. There is the test: if one factor of a system produces a mechanical, chemical or physical modification of the operation of another factor of the system, invention that is patentable may exist.

¶ 6. *Tests of these Classes*

Some of the tests determinative of novelty

---

[1] Incandescent Lamp Pat. 52 Fed. 300; 3 C. C. A. 83.
[2] Mac. Pat. § 698.
[3] Hall *v.* General, 169 Fed. 209; 94 C. C. A. 580.

mentioned in the next chapter (§ 34) may be applied here. But, in applying these tests, we must exercise care, on the one hand, not to spell invention into mere commercial success, or, on the other, by ex post facto judgment, spell obviousness into a thing, however simple, which rises above mechanical skill.[1]

[1] Mac. Pat. § 693.

CHAPTER V

PATENTABLE NOVELTY

§ 31. Novelty a Statutory Requirement

To complete this general view of the field of invention, we must consider the matter of statutory novelty in some of its aspects, and also note briefly those things which defeat it; and to do so, some analysis of § 4886 — the pivotal section of the law — must be before us. That section first makes the positive requirement that the invention must be *new*. Then follow these negative requirements:

1. Not known or used by others in this country before his invention or discovery thereof,

2. Not patented or described in any printed publication in this or any foreign country before his invention or discovery thereof or more than two years prior to his application,

3. Not in public use or on sale in this country for more than two years prior to his application,

4. Not abandoned.

Novelty means absolute novelty. If the king of the Cannibal Islands should now invent the telephone, undoubtedly it would be a novel thing to him and involve an individual act distinctly novel; but that would not be the absolute novelty the statute requires. But it may be said, this is a far-fetched illustration. Be not so sure. Every year there are thousands of cases where persons reinvent things they never heard of — novel to them, but absolutely old. I have referred to this somewhat in detail (§ 2), but it needs reiteration. Patentable novelty means that which is new compared with everything known or used previously in this country and everything patented or described by printed publication of any sort in any country. The king of the Cannibal Islands could not justify his claim for a patent by saying that he never saw the Patent Office Gazette; no more can the American who finds himself defeated by a prior description of his invention in a Chinese record plead ignorance of the language and literature of that land. The inventor must think out beyond all that has been done and known in this country and out and beyond the publications of the world.

§ 32. Things which defeat Patentable Novelty

When we turn to this negative side of the statute, we find before us the vast field of law covering anticipation, abandonment, priority, many of the main defenses which may be raised to defeat a charge of infringement, and many other subjects. These we master never; and we arrive at proficiency only after long study and experience. All that is required here, however, is a general understanding, so that the engineer or inventor may cooperate intelligently with his patent attorney, leaving to and requiring from him the knowledge and technique to deal with these problems.

¶ 1. *Prior Knowledge of or Use by Others in This Country before Invention*

Not infrequently this provision seems harsh. The Supreme Court so recognizes it,[1] and at the same time declares its absoluteness:

We must presume the patentee was fully informed of everything which preceded him, whether such were the actual fact or not. There is no doubt that the patent laws sometimes fail to do justice to

[1] Mast *v.* Stover, 177 U. S. 485; 44 L. Ed. 856; 20 S. Ct. 708.

an individual who may, with the light he had before him, have exhibited inventive talent of a high order, and yet be denied a patent by reason of antecedent devices which actually existed, but not to his knowledge, and are only revealed after a careful search in the Patent Office. But the statute (4886) is inexorable. It denies the patent if the device were known or used by others in this country before his invention. Congress having created the monopoly, may put such limitations upon it as it pleases.

But two of our great patent judges, Judge Sanborn [1] and Judge Putnam,[2] have set the proper limits to the statute application in these words:

A machine or combination which is not designed by its maker, nor actually used nor apparently adapted to perform the function of a patented machine, or combination, but which is discovered in a remote art and was used under radically different conditions to perform another function, neither anticipates nor limits the scope of the patent.

Where mechanical improvements have moved so fast as they have in the last half century, great caution is required in investigating alleged anticipations which date back nearly the whole of

[1] National v. Interchangeable, 106 Fed. 693; 45 C. C. A.; 544.
[2] Draper v. American, 161 Fed. 728; 88 C. C. A. 588.

that period; and, so far as they did not go into use, so there was no practical exhibition of them, it is often difficult to determine whether they disclosed such full, clear, and exact terms as are necessary to anticipate.

Thus we see that actual prior knowledge or use in this country is absolute, and at the same time it must be absolute in character in order to be absolute in its effects.

¶ 2. *Prior Patent or Publication in Any Country* (1) *Before the Inventive Act,* (2) *More than Two Years before Application*

(1) Patenting or publication before invention is absolutely fatal.[1] But, as in the case of prior knowledge or use in this country, — and with even greater rigor of application of the rule, — the patent or publication, especially if a foreign patent or publication, must disclose the invention so completely that it may be practiced without experiment or further invention.[2]

(2) More than two years before application. This, where there is actual invention prior to

---

[1] New Departure *v.* Bevin, 73 Fed. 469; 19 C. C. A. 534.
[2] Mac. Pat. §§ 80-85, and especially Hanifen *v.* Godshalk, 84 Fed. 649; 28 C. C. A. 507, quoted under § 85.

patent or publication, gives the inventor his two years to perfect his invention and reduce it to practice before filing his application, the same as in the next following provision.

¶ 3. *Public Use or Sale More than Two Years in this Country*

The question of public use or sale for more than two years prior to filing application for patent is not one of intent; it is a question of fact. It is not a thing to be mitigated or excused. The statute is absolute. Within the two-year limit full freedom exists. An application filed a moment inside the limit is safe; a moment later and the right is lost beyond recall. In the days of Justice Blatchford, when strict construction of the statute to defeat a patent was the habit, it was held that, when Romeo invented a corset steel and Juliet wore it next her heart for more than two years, such was public use; and also that when an invention was hidden away in the confines of a fire- and burglar-proof safe, it was public use. The question does not turn upon the number of uses or upon the number of persons concerned in the use; but it has been questioned whether a single sale would, in all cases, amount to public use.[1]

¶ 4. *Abandonment*

Loss of the right to obtain a patent, or the right to maintain the monopoly of a patent already granted, by abandonment differs from the loss of such right from public use or sale for more than two years before application is filed in that it may occur at any time — before application, after application, or even after patenting. It differs also in that it is something arising from the conduct or intent of the inventor, and not merely as a statutory limitation. Since abandonment is a forfeiture of a right, it will never be presumed; it must be proved beyond a reasonable doubt. It may be constructive — as where an inventor sits idle, and in the face of use by others, makes no effort to secure his monopoly.[2] Or it may be actual — as where there is a failure to claim the invention,[3] or where one abandons a claim in the process of Patent Office rejection and amendment.[4]

[1] Mac. Pat. pp. 67–68; see also §§ 849–858.
[2] McClurg v. Kingsland, 1 How. 202; 11 L. Ed. 102.
[3] Mac. Pat. §§ 12, 203. [4] *Ibid.*, § 207.

And here is to be noted the fact that an invention may be practically abandoned by employing an incompetent solicitor; for all that he discloses, but fails to claim, is lost. There are those who follow the line of least resistance, either because they know no better or because they lack moral rectitude. It is common practice with this class of men to draw the claims with some limiting element which will get them through the Patent Office and which, consequently, abandons any construction not so limited and containing such limiting and probably unnecessary element. Actual, conscious abandonment by an inventor is rare; but abandonment through the acts of an incompetent solicitor is common.

§ 33. Generic Invention and Improvements

There is a notion abroad that there is one rule of novelty in the case of a generic or "pioneer" invention, and another in the case of improvements. Not so. Naturally, when an invention has been established as generic, it has broad novelty; but, in order to reach this position, it must withstand far fiercer test than the modest improvement which is content with some minor distinction from its fellows. This popular notion that, if one can only endow his invention with the character of a pioneer by one means or another, he will gain some sort of immunity or some extension of his monopoly, is error.

While there may be some temporary commercial advantage in a patent which contains high-sounding and supposedly generic claims which could not be sustained, I am constrained to believe that, in the long run, such patenting is unwise. Scarecrow patents have grown less fearful, and, with the trained engineer in the field of invention, the time is near when they will be practically valueless. Moreover, such claims subject the owner to a heavy burden, if he is to keep up the bluff of his patent by suits against alleged infringers. The better course is to patent what is yours, and no more, and stand by your rights.[1]

---

[1] As an example of this practice might be cited a patent now before me, which contains upwards of one hundred claims, some of which appear on their face to be generic. As a matter of fact, this patent is in an art that is old, and aside from a half-dozen minor combinations which could have been covered by as many claims, it is lacking in patentable novelty. This patent has frightened no one; but, on the contrary, may compel the owner to bring suits where he will stand small show of success.

§ 34. Evidence and Tests of Novelty

While out of context in one sense, it will be of service to note some few evidences and tests of novelty, although most of them may be applied only after the patent is issued and has established the conditions precedent.

¶ 1. *Patent Office Action and the Patent Itself*

It is a familiar statement that the grant of a patent is prima facie evidence of novelty and patentability. And it is often said by the courts that the fact that the claims passed the scrutiny of the Patent Office is evidence of their validity. These may be proper statements; but, as a matter of fact, standing alone, these evidences count for but little. Courts rarely grant a preliminary injunction with no better showing than this bare prima facie. And yet, when it appears from the history of the application that either (1) the examiner was able to find no prior patent or publication bearing upon the claims, or (2) where the patent was allowed only after long and strenuous contest and emerged without any material limitation of the claims, — such showing is not without value.¹ But where the claims are allowed only after repeated rejection and amendment and limitation, and then only with doubt in the mind of the examiner, the showing is fairly against the patent.²

¶ 2. *Public Acquiescence*

When an invention goes on the market, drives out competitors, and stands uninfringed, such circumstances are of large influence with the court.³ But where a patent has lain dormant and made no contribution to public utility, even though it has not been infringed, the presumption is practically reversed.⁴

¶ 3. *Commercial Success and Extensive Use*

It is said that the value of a patent depends upon the amount of brains mixed with it. This is true, as it is in any other enterprise; but, as in any other enterprise, to succeed, the thing you mix with brains must have some inherent merit also. The rule of commercial success is well stated in the Collar Button Case:⁵

[1] See Mac. Pat. § 630.
[2] Smidth *v.* Bonneville, 114 Fed. 262; 52 C. C. A. 148.
[3] Wolff *v.* DuPont, 134 Fed. 862; 67 C. C. A. 488.
[4] Boston *v.* Pennsylvania, 164 Fed. 557; 90 C. C. A. 84.
[5] Krementz *v.* Cottle, 148 U. S. 556; 37 L. Ed. 558; 13 S. Ct. 719.

The argument drawn from commercial success is not always to be relied on. Other causes, such as the enterprise of the vendors and the lavish expenditures in advertising may coöperate to promote large demand. But when the facts in the case leave the question of invention in doubt, the fact that the device has gone into general use and has displaced other devices which had previously been employed for analogous uses, is sufficient to turn the scale in favor of the existence of invention.

And the Barbed Wire Case,[1] to which we shall refer more fully in connection with the last step rule (¶ 5 below) fixes the value of extensive use as probative of novelty.

But this rule has been overworked. In many cases judges have found it an easy way to steady a wabbling judgment; and the Supreme Court in the Rubber Tire Case[2] applied this rule, and at the same time clearly distinguished it as a matter of evidence from judicial doubt or inertia.

¶ 4. *Efficiency and Utility*

These are tests kindred to commercial success and extensive use. The test of efficiency came into

---

[1] 143 U. S. 275; 36 L. Ed. 154; 12 S. Ct. 443.
[2] Diamond *v.* Consolidated, 220 U. S. 428; 55 L. Ed. 527; 31 S. Ct. 444.

play in the old Loom Case.¹ In that case the patent disclosed no single, marked improvement, but a series of minor improvements which, taken together, increased the efficiency of the carpet loom from forty yards per day in the hands of a skilled workman to fifty yards per day in the hands of an unskilled workman. This fact, taken with others, saved the patent.

The utility rule has been well stated by Judge Ward in a comparatively recent case:[2]

Has the patentee added anything of value to the sum of human knowledge, has he made the world's work easier, cheaper, safer, would the return to the prior art be a retrogression? When the court has answered this question, or these questions, in the affirmative, the effort should be made to give the inventor the just reward of the contribution he has made. The effort should increase in proportion as the contribution is valuable. Where the court has to deal with a device which has achieved undisputed success and accomplishes a result never attained before, which is new, useful and in large demand, it is generally safe to conclude that the man who made it is an inventor.

[1] Loom Co. *v.* Higgins, 105 U. S. 580; 26 L. Ed. 1177.
[2] O'Rourke *v.* McMullen, 160 Fed. 933; 88 C. C. A. 115.

¶ 5. *Prior Failures — Last Step Rule*

The inventor who turns prior failures into success has his patent fortified by a long list of decisions.[1] These we cannot review, but we may illustrate this rule and also the last step rule by the Barbed Wire Case.[2] Since we shall have occasion to refer to this case again, we will go into the facts somewhat fully.

With the settling-up of the great western plains, fencing became a great problem. There was little timber, and to make a wire fence that would turn a Texas steer was no easy task. Up to the time of Glidden, the patentee of the barbed wire that succeeded, the nearest to success was that of the Kelly patent, shown in the annexed drawing of the patent.

This was a reasonably good fence, but it would not turn cattle, at least not the range cattle of the West; and, consequently, farmers would not buy it. Then came Glidden with the fence shown in the annexed drawings of that patent.

---

[1] Mac. Pat. §§ 631, 633.
[2] 143 U. S. 275; 36 L. Ed. 154; 12 S. Ct. 443.

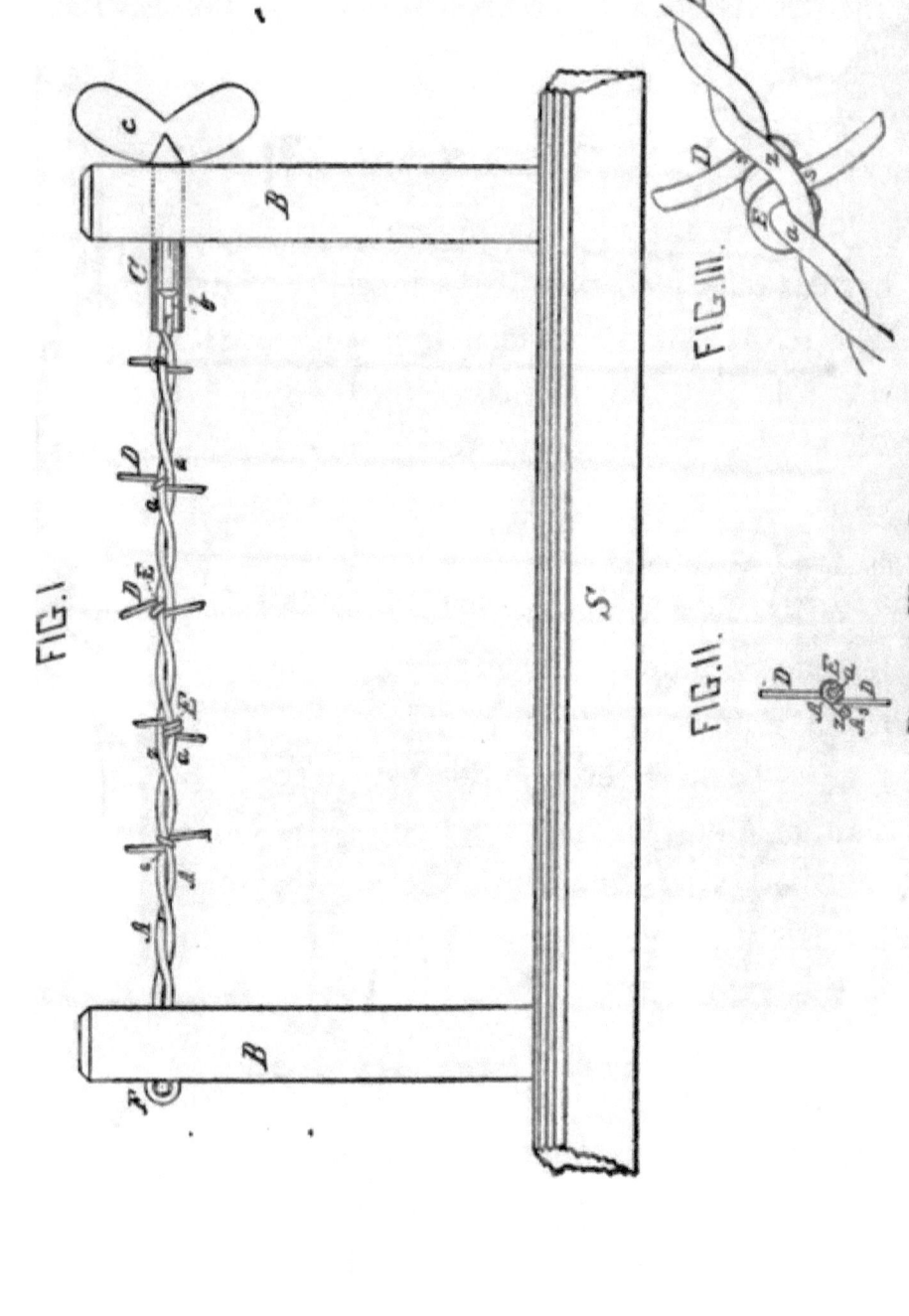

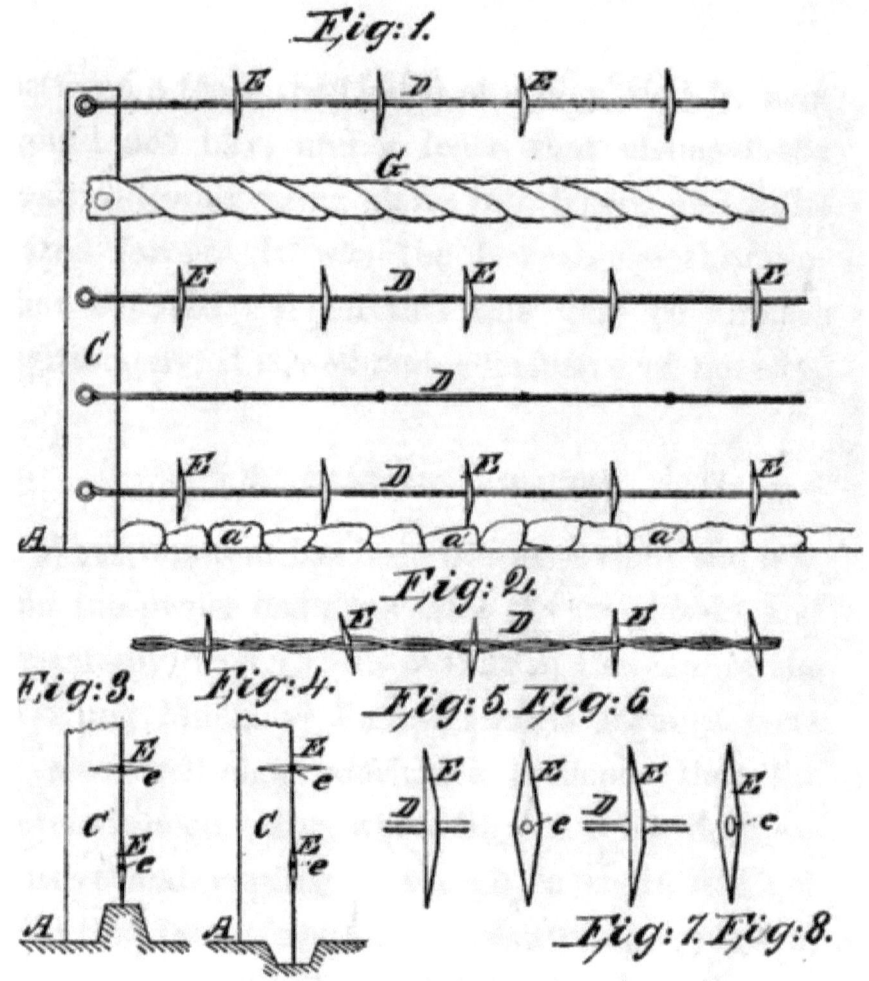

KELLY WIRE FENCE PATENT

It is at once clear that the step from Kelly to Glidden is short; but it marked the difference between a fence that would not turn a Texas steer and one that would. It marked the difference between a fence that failed of utility, that farmers would not buy, and a fence that changed the prairies from grazing plains into fenced and cultivated farms. It was the last step — the step that counted. When this rule may be applied legitimately, it is well-nigh conclusive of novelty.

¶ 6. *Extensive Litigation*

When a patent has been infringed right and left, and the owner has gone after the trespassers and repeatedly driven them out, as in the case of the Washing Machine[1] Patent, such a state of facts is also well-nigh conclusive evidence that the patent is good. But where litigation has been extensive and varying in success, a court will not hold that fact as necessarily negativing invention, as did the Circuit Court of Appeals in the Rubber Tire Case,[2] and it may hold that fact as evidence

---

[1] Wayne *v.* Benbow-Brammer, 168 Fed. 271; 93 C. C. A. 573.

[2] Consolidated *v.* Diamond, 162 Fed. 892; 89 C. C. A. 582.

of invention, as did the Supreme Court on the appeal of that case.[1]

¶ 7. *Attempted Evasion*

Akin to extensive litigation is attempted evasion. It must be some evidence of invention when people are so desirous of using the device that they make clumsy efforts to avoid the patent — evidence both of novelty and utility; and the clumsiness or poor success in evading the patent leads one to think that something more than mechanical skill has been exercised.[2]

¶ 8. *Use by Defendant*

Of course, use by defendant is good evidence of utility; for it does not lie in his mouth to say in one breath, I am using the device, and in the next that the device is useless; and often this is also strong evidence of novelty.[3] But when both complainant and defendant have patents, this rule may become a boomerang, if the complainant has

---

[1] 220 U. S. 428; 55 L. Ed. 527; 31 S. Ct. 444.
[2] Heap *v.* Tremont, 82 Fed. 449; 27 C. C. A. 316.
[3] Gandy *v.* Main, 143 U. S. 587; 36 L. Ed. 272; 12 S. Ct. 598; Brammer *v.* Schroeder, 106 Fed. 918; 46 C. C. A. 41.

made no use of his patent and the defendant has used his with commercial success.[1]

While these several tests are mere evidence — never conclusive proof of novelty — they are valuable in measuring out justice; and their recital shows how the courts use common sense in dealing with patents. It will also shed some light upon the following subjects.

[1] Raymond *v.* Keystone, 134 Fed. 866; 67 C. C. A. 492.

CHAPTER VI

THE OBTAINING OF PATENTS

§ 35. Introductory

THIS chapter is not a treatise on patent soliciting. This must be distinctly understood. It is commonly supposed by the inexperienced that the mere soliciting of a patent is a simple matter; that it involves no more than procuring a copy of the Patent Office Rules, following the rules and forms, and getting the application through. Probably a majority of patents are obtained in about this way, and that is one reason why the average patent is of small value. But a fact to be emphasized with all vigor is this:

The Patent Office, generally, will see to it that you do not claim more than you should; but THE PATENT OFFICE IS ABSOLUTELY UNCONCERNED AS TO WHETHER YOUR INVENTION IS PROTECTED.

The drawing of a patent application is not, primarily or chiefly, a matter of engineering; it is primarily and chiefly a matter of patent law.

Many inventors and some engineers think they can best solicit their own patents, or even that their knowledge of engineering and mechanics fits them for soliciting patents for others. Any patent attorney of experience knows how often such work results either in getting the application in a tangle or in securing claims that give little or no protection.

It is quite enough for an engineer to know his own science. I have small patience with the engineer or inventor who thinks he knows all of the science of the patent law as a mere incident and side-issue to his profession; and I have absolutely no patience whatever with the patent attorney who presumes to be past-master of the field of engineering. Both kinds exist — in small numbers, I am glad to say.

As has been said, the work of the engineer and patent attorney should be team work. One should supplement the other. The best drawn patents are thus obtained.

§ 36. Attorneys and Solicitors

A patent attorney and a patent solicitor are two distinct individuals. While most patent attorneys are also patent solicitors, only a portion of the patent solicitors doing business are admitted attorneys with general training in the law. The Patent Office Rules permit any one to solicit his own patent, and permit almost any one to become a patent solicitor. He need not be a lawyer and is not required to possess any great degree of engineering knowledge. There is a great army of patent solicitors possessing varied abilities and degrees of training; and while it does not in the least follow that, in order to be a good solicitor, one must be a practicing attorney, it does follow that, owing to the laxness of the rules, the majority of incompetent solicitors are those who are mere solicitors.

And here arise two views of patent soliciting. One may look at it merely in the light of getting a patent; or one may have in mind the securing of claims which will stand the test of time and litigation. The first is the view that dominates the mere solicitor who is in the business to solicit as many patents and get as many fees as he can. The second view is the one which should dominate the true solicitor; and it matters not whether he is lawyer or solicitor, trained or untrained, if his mind is on the fee instead of the claim, he is to be shunned.

Let it be understood that in passing this somewhat harsh criticism, I am not directing it against any worthy solicitor or attorney, but against those individuals who make soliciting a mere money pursuit like the quack doctor, and particularly against those advertising concerns who run patent factories.

Again it is to be remarked that none of us can live up to the high standard we would like; for we all have to solicit patents for clients who insist upon having a patent of some sort. The blame for small patents, patents possessing no novelty, does not reside alone with the solicitors; for quite as often it is the manufacturer who wants a scarecrow or the man who invents patents instead of patenting inventions.

§ 37. Selecting a Patent Attorney

It therefore follows that, whether you employ a patent attorney or a patent solicitor, you should see to it, first of all, that he views the undertaking with reference to obtaining a patent which will stand the ordeal, not only of litigation, but which, upon examination by the most expert to determine whether it may be infringed with impunity, will pass the ordeal and *prevent litigation.* The attorney who thus advises you may decide against filing an application; or, upon the showing of anticipating references, may advise you to abandon an application already filed.

In the second place, bear in mind the fact that you want a patent attorney in personal touch with you, rather than in personal touch with the Patent Office. There is a foolish idea most prevalent that a Washington solicitor can get the ear of an examiner and secure results that a non-resident attorney cannot. All business with the Patent Office must be transacted in writing,[1] and

> The personal attendance of applicants at the Patent Office is unnecessary. Their business can be transacted by correspondence.[2]

Even the Washington solicitor, who may see the examiner personally, has to put his amendments and arguments in writing and await his regular turn with all the others, even though he may have presented the subject personally.

---

[1] P. O. Rule 1.   [2] *Ibid.,* Rule 4.

Moreover, most good patent attorneys have associates in Washington — men of character and men who are respected by the examiners — who are abundantly able to present most matters requiring personal conference. And it is only on rare occasions that a solicitor need go to the examiner. When such occasion arises, the non-resident attorney is given every courtesy upon making regular appointment.

Hence, put your patent work in the hands of an attorney of established reputation who will charge you, not a flat minimum price, but who will charge according to the amount of labor involved. Employ an attorney who is available for personal conference, if possible. Work with him and place the responsibility upon him.

§ 38. When Application should be Filed

There is a very common notion that, immediately one invents something, he must file a patent application, else his invention may be stolen or in some way jeopardized. Let us get this right. In the first place the statute gives the inventor two years of actual public use of the invention before his right to apply for a patent becomes abandoned.[1] Hence, so far as the legal right to make application is concerned, there is no need of undue haste. In the second place, the time in which the invention is in process of experimentation and development, if it is truly experimental and developmental, is additional to the two years' public use.[2] But one may not abuse this two-year right; for if the machine or process is essentially perfect, the fact that minor details are not completed or that the inventor wishes to make various additions and improvements will not save an invention from abandonment if thus used for more than two years.[3] In the third place, it must be remembered that it is the date of invention and reduction to practice which determines priority, and not the filing date of the application. But unless the invention is reduced to practice, the filing date is of importance, as ruled in Automatic v. Pneumatic.[4]

In these circumstances, then, what should be

[1] R. S. 4886.
[2] Elizabeth v. American, 97 U. S. 126; 24 L. Ed. 1000; American v. Mills, 149 Fed. 743; 79 C. C. A. 449.
[3] Swain v. Holyoke, 109 Fed. 154; 48 C. C. A. 265; Jenner v. Bowen, 139 Fed. 556; 71 C. C. A. 540; National v. Lambert, 142 Fed. 164; 73 C. C. A. 382.
[4] Automatic v. Pneumatic, 166 Fed. 288; 92 C. C. A. 206.

done? The first self-evident thing is, not to rush to your attorney the moment an idea presents itself, but to perform the second requirement of the statute and reduce it to practice in some form. Not only should this be done to comply with the statute, but rushing an application in before it has been matured properly is very often a most unfortunate thing. To illustrate: An inventor lays before me the drawings and data for an application upon an improvement in certain machinery. The application is filed, and some time thereafter, as the result of further study and observation, the inventor finds that a certain feature, partially shown in the drawings and inadequately described in the specification, when properly developed, becomes one of the most vital features of the invention. There is trouble on either hand. To make this feature a part of the application filed necessitates revision of the drawings, specification, and the writing of new claims. And this, of course, necessitates a supplemental oath in which the inventor must swear that the subject-matter added was a part of the original invention — a justifiable course in some cases, but one which is generally unwelcome to the examiner. To file a second application, in addition to the expense, presents new troubles. Had the invention been thoroughly reduced to practice, these conditions would not have existed.

It is part of the game played by advertising solicitors to keep up the idea that an invention must be patented at once in order to protect it; and I regret to have to add that it is far too common for attorneys generally to assent by silence, if not otherwise, to this idea of immediate haste. Where the haste should be is in properly reducing the invention to practice, by getting it on paper, studying it, criticizing it, and if need be, building it to make sure of its practicality.

On the other hand, when an invention is actually ready for application, little delay should be permitted. Only two reasons need be stated: First, filing of application is at least constructive reduction to practice, and if one has not made actual physical reduction, under the rule of Automatic *v.* Pneumatic, *supra*, another inventor, inventing later but reducing his invention to practice physically, may be held to be the prior inventor. Second, delay always increases the chances of being the junior party in an interference. This puts the burden of proof upon the party last filing, and so he has the up-hill work in an interference contest.

Then there is another notion held by many. It is that if they take the full two years allowed by the statute before making application, they can prolong the life of the patent. So they can, but to what purpose? The patent is good for seventeen years, and any inventor who cannot make all there is to be made out of an invention in these days of rapid progress is not likely to make at all. One inventor might be instanced who has followed this practice of delay of application for twenty years in the face of all advice and protest, with the result that he has been defeated in one interference by reason of his delay, and the further result that he has lost one of the most valuable inventions of these twenty years by exceeding the two-year limit.

To sum up is hardly necessary. A sentence does it: Reduce your invention to practice — either on paper or in physical form — and having done so, file the application.

§ 39. Searches and Preliminary Examinations

It is common practice to have a search or preliminary examination to determine whether an invention is novel. This work is done usually by an experienced searcher in Washington. The Patent Office will not make a search or give any information as to patentability in advance of the filing and examination of an application.[1] And any attempt to make a search from the index and files of the Patent Office Gazette is worse than useless.

A thorough preliminary examination, made by a competent searcher, is generally valuable; *but it is never conclusive of novelty.* What the searcher does is to go through the subclasses that contain similar inventions. Usually he sends copies of patents most nearly like the thing in hand, and leaves the attorney to determine the question of patentability.

But such a search has serious limitations. First, it covers only the United States patents. It does not cover the foreign art, nor does it cover any prior publication excepting the United States

---

[1] P. O. Rule 14.

patents. Second, it does not cover, and, of course, cannot cover, pending applications in the Patent Office. Third, it is never certain that the subclasses examined cover all that there is in the Patent Office that may anticipate. The classification is coming to be excellent, but it is far from perfect; and it is common experience to have a patent cited by the examiner which a conscientious and careful searcher failed to discover. Fourth, the value of a search varies directly with the ability and thoroughness of the searcher. It goes without saying that a "free" search, such as unscrupulous solicitors offer, is utterly worthless; and the ordinary two or three dollar search is of relatively small value. Fifth, in a highly complex art, such, for example, as railway signaling; or in processes or compositions of matter, a search that costs less than the full filing cost of an application has small determinative value. Sixth, two other things may happen: the best searcher may overlook a perfectly clear anticipation, or a patent which is a perfect anticipation may have been abstracted from the files at the time the search was made. Both of these are within my experience.

Then what should the inventor do? The answer is simple. Have a search made by a first-class man, paying a reasonable price for it. When you get it, take the position that it *proves nothing unless it proves anticipation*. It is a purely negative test. If it does not prove anticipation, file your application with the foreknowledge that the examiner — with both domestic and foreign art before him, and, generally, special familiarity with the art to which it relates — is likely to dig up anticipatory matter you never dreamed of.

§ 40. Preparing a Case for the Patent Attorney

Conditions are so various that no general rule can be laid down. In simple cases a sketch, photograph, model or working drawings, with proper description may be quite sufficient to enable the attorney to proceed; but it is to be observed that, as a rule, working drawings without assembled views are undesirable. The patent drawing is a picture, rather than a drawing; its purpose is to disclose the machine with reference to its mode of operation, and not to furnish drawings from which it may be constructed directly.

The inventor should assume that the attorney knows nothing of the art to which the invention relates. This course will make the inventor thorough in describing his device and in pointing out its novel features, and will make certain the points the attorney wishes to know. There is another advantage in the doing of this: It happens not infrequently that, in dictating or writing out a description of a set of drawings, a defect will be discovered and corrected before the work leaves the inventor's hands. It is well, also, to conclude such a description with enumeration of the points it is desired to secure by claim.

Unless one has a draftsman thoroughly familiar with making Patent Office drawings, it is inadvisable to attempt them. The patent attorney will prepare the most advantageous views for disclosing the invention and laying the foundation for the claims he will draw.

§ 41. The Parts of the Application

While these are matters which should be left to the attorney, the engineer or inventor should know, in general, of what they consist. A complete application embraces the following parts:

(1) Petition, (2) Power of Attorney, (3) Specification, (4) Claims, (5) Oath, (6) Drawings, when the case permits.

¶ 1. *The Petition*

The petition is a communication addressed to the Commissioner of Patents, setting forth matters of citizenship, residence and post-office address, asking for the grant of a patent upon the invention named and set forth in the accompanying papers. This and all other papers should follow, as nearly as possible, the forms prescribed by the Patent Office. The Patent Office Rules, which may be had free of charge by addressing the Commissioner of Patents, contain, in addition to all rules of the office, forms and fee lists. This, and a copy of the Patent Laws, which may be had in like manner, should be in the hands of applicant or engineer; and I refer the reader to those pamphlets for all the numerous details which are here omitted.

¶ 2. *The Power of Attorney*

This empowers the person to whom it is given, whether he be an attorney or not as long as he is a registered solicitor, to prosecute the application, make alterations, amendments, arguments and receive the patent when issued. It is a revokable power, but while in force gives the attorney exclusive control of the application. An assignment of the entire interest in an application and its recording in the Patent Office does not revoke the power, but it enables the assignee to revoke it at any time after recording, and to substitute another attorney. But the attorney has no power to file a new oath or a supplemental oath executed by himself,[1] nor can he verify a preliminary statement in an interference.[2]

¶ 3. *The Specification*

The term "specification" may prove somewhat confusing to the beginner in reading court decisions. He will find the early decisions using the term as covering both the description and the claims, and in one or two early decisions he will find the court speaking of the claim as if it were the specification. In the later decisions he will find the courts using the term "specification" as covering the descriptive portion exclusive of the claims.

[1] R. S. §§ 4892, 4895; P. O. Rule 48.
[2] P. O. Rule 110.

Properly speaking, the "specification" covers and includes: (1) preamble, (2) general statement of object and nature of the invention, (3) brief description of views of drawings, (4) detailed description, (5) claims, (6) signature of inventor, (7) signatures of two witnesses.[1]

While recognizing the technical correctness of this rule, since the claims are of such vital moment and are subject to rules so radically different from those governing the description, I shall follow the common practice of treating them separately.

¶ 4. *The Claims*

..... And he shall particularly point out and distinctly claim the part, improvement, or combination which he claims as his invention or discovery.[2]

Since I shall devote an entire chapter to the subject of the claim (§§ 53–67), nothing more need be said here.

¶ 5. *The Oath*

Follow the statute absolutely by following the form in the Patent Office Rules. You may take liberties at some points, but not here. While the

---

[1] P. O. Rule 39.   [2] R. S. § 4888.

courts will disregard all ordinary errors in the specification, and will even deal leniently with a clumsily drawn claim, they have no choice when it comes to the oath. The statute prescribes what the applicant must swear to in order to secure the patent grant. There is, however, little chance of a defective oath escaping the scrutiny of the Patent Office, but no chances should be taken.

¶ 6. *The Drawings*

The statute provides that drawings shall be furnished whenever the case admits, and that they shall be annexed to and form a part of the patent.[1] The purpose and object of the drawings cannot be better stated than in the two following quotations:[2]

The object of the drawings filed in the Patent Office is attained if they clearly exhibit the principles involved, and, in a case like this, rigid adherence to the dimensions thus exhibited is not required or expected, and if the intelligent mechanic would so proportion the dimensions as to secure practical results, inutility is not dem-

---

[1] R. S. §§ 4884, 4889.
[2] Crown *v.* Aluminum, 108 Fed. 845; 48 C. C. A. 72; Western *v.* American, 131 Fed. 75; 65 C. C. A. 313.

onstrated by experiments with material identical in form and proportion of parts with the drawings in the patent.

The drawings are not required to be working plans, they must be read in connection with the description and claims, and any inference arising from omissions or inconsistencies in the drawings must yield to a legally sufficient specification.

§ 42. Examination

The application having been prepared, executed and filed, together with the fee required by the statute, the papers are examined, and if found in proper condition of form and completeness, the application is given a filing date and serial number. Thereafter the application is always identified by its date and serial number, together with the name of applicant and the title of invention, until it issues as a patent and is given a date of issue and a patent number. The serial number and the patent number are distinct, and never the same.

Assigned to its proper division and room, the application then awaits its turn, like a patient at a clinic; and when it is reached, it is put through an examination the thoroughness of which is little appreciated. We need not go into the details of these examinations further than to say that, from the first line of the petition to the last detail of the drawings, nothing is taken for granted. Every minor error — even the transposition of two letters in a word by the typewriter — is noted as an error and stated in the action.

The examination as to novelty is the most thorough of any patent office in the world; and, considering the pressure upon the examiners, the ever-increasing volume and ever-increasing complexity of the more important arts, it is remarkable that the examination comes so near a finality. But it never is, and in the nature of things never can be, a finality. The most and best that it ever can be is a reasonably close approximation to the determination of actual novelty.[1]

§ 43. The First Action

The first action, in addition to calling attention to all informal matters, discloses defects in speci-

---

[1] Since I am addressing engineers, and since no class is more concerned with the proper and efficient working of the Patent Office, it is proper to note some suggestions which are the result of experience and observation. In the reform and betterment of our patent system engineers should take an active part, individually and through their various societies.

We have periodic outbursts in the press and in Congress charging awful laxness in our Patent Office. Assigning proper

fication and drawings which are vital, deals vigorously with construction and phraseology of the

share to blatant reporters muck-raking for news and to representatives with ideas of reform out of all proportion to their knowledge of facts, there is left some considerable ground for criticism. I shall suggest two lines of action which would result in large increase in efficiency, and consequent reduction of legitimate criticism.

First, a very simple, practical and immediate reform. The fee on filing an application is $15. The final fee when the application goes to issue is $20. The cost of a copy of any patent is 5 cents. Subscription to the Patent Office Gazette is $5 per year. Suppose we reverse the filing and final fees, making the filing fee $20 and the final fee $15, thus adding nothing to the cost of a patent. This would add to the income of the office $5 on every application made but not prosecuted to issue — amounting to over $275,000. The cost of a copy of a patent should not be less than ten cents, and would then be cheaper than in any other country. Any private corporation attempting to publish the Patent Office Gazette for a subscription fee of $5 per year would bankrupt in short order. Ten dollars a year is less than the cost of any law publication of similar dimensions — vastly less. These obvious and proper changes would increase the annual income sufficiently to add at least fifty examiners and their complement of clerks and stenographers; and this would be without the least increase of burden upon the real inventor, but with some discouragement to inconsequential applications.

Second, with accumulated earnings amounting to nearly $7,000,000, the Patent Office should have a building and equipment which would increase the efficiency of the working force enormously. Such increase in efficiency can be had by using these earnings properly and without increase of burden upon the Federal treasury.

Third, going to the vital point directly, the statute says, "Any person who has invented or discovered any new *and useful* art, machine," etc. The examination in the Patent Office is directed so exclusively to the question of novelty claims, and discloses the prior art as found which is anticipatory of any claim.

The claims are read as presented — not as they may be restricted or amended — and the action is *never constructive*. It is always critical. It is a regrettable fact that the departmental style and form is generally Rooseveltian, sometimes Napoleonic, and occasionally bulldozing. But this is

that it may be said there is no examination as to utility at all. In this respect the Patent Office has been conducted all these years in a manner tantamount to violation of the fundamental law. Only in cases of palpable inoperativeness or in the case of an application which, if patented, would be in contravention of good morals is the question of utility given any consideration. Again the statute says: (§ 4893)

On the filing of any such application and the payment of the fees required by law, the Commissioner of Patents shall cause an examination to be made of the alleged new invention or discovery; and if on such examination it shall appear that the claimant is justly entitled to a patent under the law, *and the same is sufficiently useful and important*, the Commissioner shall issue a patent therefor.

This gives the Commissioner power, not only to pass upon the question of utility, but the importance — *or insignificance* — of an application.

But it will at once be said that to put inventors at the mercy of the Patent Office by leaving to its discretion the questions of usefulness and importance of all invention would be to make fallible human judgment, preconception, guesswork, or caprice controlling. And there is also the objection that it is **impossible, in many cases**, to reach any judgment as to the future utility of an invention. These objections have their weight, and, of course, such a rule could be applied only to those cases where the want of utility or utter unimportance is evident and indisputable. But with every doubt to be resolved **in favor of the applicant**, and the right to present

mere departmental habit and tradition. The examiners are mortals doing their duty to the utmost of their ability, dealing with applicants and attorneys entirely unknown to them; and always in a critical and destructive frame of mind — necessarily so, for they stand between the public and the army of inventors and attorneys who are constantly seeking the earth and the contents thereof without respect to what is their due. At times this dogmatism of the examiners leads to the feeling that the Patent Office is run for the sole purpose of defeating meritorious claims. Not so. With the exception of a single examiner, who has long since gone hence, I never have known a case of real hostility to inventors in general.

proofs and the right of appeal secured to him, it is clear that no greater objection lies than that which applies with equal force to the present system of determining patentable novelty. And it is self-evident to those who are familiar with the mass of useless material going into the Patent Office every year that such a rule, even most conservatively applied, could not fail to eliminate thousands of applications otherwise maturing into patents of no value whatever.

With the enormous accumulation of inconsequential patents which hamper progress and menace the engineer on every hand, some such course is becoming an absolute necessity. It is a necessity already in order to give a valid and important patent the standing it should have with the courts, that it may be protected against infringement short of protracted and expensive litigation.

The action is always laconic, and is to be read and studied with care. Should the examiners enter upon explanation and argument as to their rulings, discussion and controversy would be endless. Hence their brief statements are to be taken as conclusions merely, the reasons for which the applicant is to infer or discover.

§ 44. Amendment or Argument after First Action

Before responding to the first action of the examiner, the attorney will have before him all of the references cited, and will have submitted them and a copy of the action to his client. This he certainly will do if his client is an engineer or a man of training and experience; and he will ask him to examine the action and the references and make such suggestions as may be helpful in responding.

Here is where the engineer and attorney can do team work of the highest order; where the combined abilities will put before the examiner statements and arguments which he must recognize and accept.

Various conditions may exist. One claim may be squarely anticipated; another may be found, when read in the light of a reference, to be stated too broadly — so broadly as to cover more than was intended; another claim may be clearly distinguishable from the reference. In any case, keep in mind three facts: First, the examiner is not seeking to deprive you of a substantial right. Second, the examiner means, when he rejects a claim upon a reference (unless it appears that the alleged invention is wholly anticipated) that the reference anticipates the claim *as it stands*, not as it may be amended. Third, if he has rejected a claim on a reference that is without bearing, it is possible that your specification has failed to disclose the invention properly.

Since the applicant has a year from the date of any action within which to amend or reply, the response should not be hasty or ill-considered. This is particularly true of actions in response to first actions; for it is my observation that upon the response to the first action more depends than is commonly supposed. Failure at this point will be overcome later only with much difficulty. On the other hand, do not defer action until the last moment. It prejudices the case in the eye of the examiner, especially so in view of the severe criticism of the Selden Case.

It is futile to insist upon a claim that is squarely met. In my opinion it is futile to attempt to cover the same thing or the same combination by circumlocution of phraseology. In this I do not expect full agreement; for it is the belief of many attorneys that it is expedient to get claims as broad as possible, regardless of whether they would stand the test of litigation. Either a claim is anticipated or else it is not. If it is anticipated, I see no purpose of having it in a patent, where it must be disclaimed in order that the owner may recover damages or costs.[1] If the claim is not squarely anticipated, there is no reason why it should not be redrawn to avoid the reference and the distinction made plain to the examiner.

This subject is further considered in connection with claim analysis and construction (§§ 53–65).

§ 45. Subsequent Actions and Amendments

As a rule, after the first action and response, the struggle dwindles to a series of compromises. Most examiners recede from untenable positions gracefully and promptly, as they should; but some do so only under compulsion, and occasionally only

[1] Mac. Pat. §§ 340–344.

after much discussion and persuasion. It is quite the fashion with attorneys to regard an examiner as an invidious individual who is a mere clerk in the employ of the Government, and it is also quite the fashion for an examiner to regard himself as a judicial officer who ought to be regarded with all the deference and salaam due to a judge. Both are wrong, but the examiner is more nearly right. The examiner holds a position of high responsibility, and should be treated accordingly. On the other hand, the examiner should be big enough and broad enough to eliminate his personality in according to an inventor his just rights.

At this stage of proceedings one of two conditions should be evident: either the application is worth prosecution with all possible vigor, or else it is valueless and should be dropped. Naturally, an attorney dislikes to confess to his client that he cannot get a respectable claim, and generally an inventor is loth to abandon a once bright hope. But where is the gain in fighting facts? Here the engineer should differentiate himself from the inventor following a forlorn hope. An invention or a patent is but an incident in his calling. If he finds his application defeated or so limited as to have no practical value, he should be large enough to charge it up to experience and go about his business.

§ 46. Interferences

One of the possible events during the pendency of application and after issue of the patent is an interference.

An interference is a proceeding instituted for the purpose of determining the question of priority of invention between two or more parties claiming substantially the same patentable invention. The fact that one of the parties has already obtained a patent will not prevent an interference, for, although the Commissioner has no power to cancel a patent, he may grant another patent for the same invention to a person who proves to be the prior inventor.[1]

The nine different conditions under which an interference will be declared need not be enumerated.[2] Nor will any attempt be made to describe the practice and procedure.

There is no more obsolete, unwieldy, technical, unreasonable practice or procedure known to the

---

[1] P. O. Rule 93; R. S. § 4904.
[2] P. O. Rule 94.

law than that which is employed to determine the simple question of fact — which of two inventors is entitled to a patent. It is the one disgrace of our patent system. By dilatory motions, appeals, endless traveling over the country taking testimony and appeal after appeal, a wealthy and unscrupulous person or corporation can tire out and wear down a worthy but impecunious contestant.

Of course, in an ordinary case, the contest need be neither long nor expensive; but it should be impressed upon engineers, inventors and manufacturers that they should array themselves on the side of the revolt that is now arising against this atrocious and archaic system. To say less upon this subject would be to ignore a grave evil; to say more would be to enter upon a technical subject of little interest to one not immediately concerned.

§ 47. Allowance and Issue

When an application has passed the ordeal of the office, a formal notice of allowance is sent to the attorney for applicant. The final fee must be paid within six months from the date of this notice, else the application forfeits for nonpayment of final fee. The patent issues the fourth Tuesday following the payment of the final fee.

The Patent Office Gazette of the week of issue contains a view from the drawings and a portion of the claims, together with the name and address of the patentee; and this opens the way for practices which should be mentioned.

Immediately one becomes a patentee he is the mark for all sorts of advertising sharks — advertising solicitors who are willing to do wonderful things for nothing; others who will procure patents in foreign countries for a song; others who are ready to buy the patent for cash; others who will sell it for a fabulous sum. As I write this paragraph a letter from a client lies before me, saying that he has a communication from one of these fakirs who states that he has a German manufacturer who wants to buy the German right to the invention just patented. That communication on its face brands the man a knave or a fool; for the invention is not patented in Germany and cannot be patented there because the right has expired.

Have a waste-basket handy at such times. The fact that scores of these sharks thrive at all times justifies this warning.

§ 48. Abandoned and Forfeited Applications

An abandoned application is one which has failed of completion within one year from the date of filing, or which has failed of prosecution for a year following any action, or which has been expressly abandoned in writing.[1]

A forfeited application is one which has failed of payment of the final fee within six months from allowance and notice of such fact.[2]

An abandoned application may be renewed by the inventor, who must file anew all parts of the application except a model, in case one has been filed with the original application.[3]

A forfeited application may be revived at any time within two years from the date of the notice of allowance, upon payment of a second initial fee; and such revival may be made by the inventor or by the assignee of an interest therein.[4] Such revived application, as in the case of an abandoned application, will be viewed from the date of revival and not the original filing date;[5] and the

---

[1] P. O. Rule 171; R. S. § 4894.
[2] P. O. Rule 174.
[3] *Ibid.*, Rule 173.
[4] *Ibid.*, Rule 175; R. S. § 4897.
[5] P. O. Rule 176.

question of abandonment will be considered as a question of fact.

§ 49. Application by Executor, Administrator, or Committee

In the event of the death of an inventor prior to the filing of an application for patent, or in the event of his insanity prior to filing, the statute [1] gives his executor, administrator or committee the power to make application in his place and stead, upon proof of the fact and due appointment of such legal representative.

§ 50. Disclaimer

The statutes make the following provisions for a disclaimer.[2]

Whenever, through inadvertence, accident, or mistake, and without fraudulent or deceptive intention, a patentee has claimed more than that of which he was the original and first inventor or discoverer, his patent shall be valid for all that part which is truly and justly his own, provided the same is a material and substantial part of the thing patented; and any such patentee, his heirs or assigns, whether of the whole or any sectional

---

[1] R. S. § 4896.   [2] *Ibid.*, §§ 4917, 973.

interest therein, may, on payment of the fee required by law, make disclaimer of such parts of the thing patented as he shall not choose to claim or to hold by virtue of the patent or assignment, stating therein the extent of his interest in such patent. Such disclaimer shall be in writing, attested by one or more witnesses, and recorded in the Patent Office; and it shall thereafter be considered as part of the original specification to the extent of the interest possessed by the claimant and by those claiming under him after the record thereof. But no such disclaimer shall affect any action pending at the time of its being filed, except so far as may relate to the question of unreasonable neglect or delay in filing it.

When judgment or decree is rendered for the plaintiff or complainant, in any suit at law or in equity, for the infringement of a part of a patent, in which it appears that the patentee, in his specification, claimed to be the original and first inventor or discoverer of any material or substantial part of the thing patented, of which he was not the original and first inventor, no costs shall be recovered, unless the proper disclaimer, as provided by the patent laws, has been entered at the Patent Office before the suit was brought.

The difference between a disclaimer and a reissue is that the former limits and the latter corrects. This is the broad distinction, although a reissue may also operate as a disclaimer. The object of a disclaimer is to enable the patentee to avoid having his patent fail under the statutory defenses.

It is a rule held to in some circuits, but not in others, that where one claim is found valid and infringed and another void for anticipation, that a final decree awarding injunction and accounting will not be entered until after disclaimer of the void claim is filed.[1] This I consider an unsettled question, which should be passed upon by the Supreme Court.

§ 51. Reissues

The scope and purpose of a reissue cannot be stated more clearly and tersely than in the language of the statute:[2]

Whenever any patent is inoperative or invalid, by reason of a defective or insufficient specification, or by reason of the patentee claiming as his own invention or discovery more than he had a right to claim as new, if the error has arisen by inadvertence, accident, or mistake, and without any fraudulent or deceptive intention, the Com-

---

[1] Mac. Pat. § 344.   [2] R. S. § 4916.

missioner shall, on surrender of such patent and the payment of the duty required by law, cause a new patent for the same invention, and in accordance with the corrected specification, to be issued to the patentee, or, in case of his death or of an assignment of the whole or any undivided part of the original patent, then to his executors, administrators, or assigns, for the unexpired part of the term of the original patent. Such surrender shall take effect upon the issue of the amended patent. . . . .

Notwithstanding the perfect clearness of this statement, no section of the patent statute has been the cause of so much subversion and controversy.

It is the common notion, even shared by some attorneys, that a patent may always be reissued to cure any defect. Such is not the law. It was never the purpose of this act to permit the patentee to extend his monopoly by broadening his claim, nor was it intended as a means of relief to him who procures any sort of a patent and delays correcting it to suit his convenience or when infringement arises. After long and weary wandering, this prodigal has returned, and the story of his travels may be summed up thus:[1]

---

[1] The authorities establishing the first ten rules above given are Miller v. Brass Co. 104 U. S. 350; 26 L. Ed. 783;

1. The reissue cannot cover another invention than that of the original.

2. It cannot cover what was described but not claimed after long delay.

3. While a reissue claim may be enlarged, this can be done only where actual mistake has occurred, and then only without delay.

4. To enlarged claims the rule of laches [1] applies rigorously.

5. The purpose of the statute is to enable the inventor to correct mistakes, and not to extend or prolong the monopoly.

6. Diligence must be had, a delay of two years will be treated as evidence, though not conclusive, of abandonment.

7. The question of reasonableness of delay is generally a question of law for the court.

Topliff v. Topliff, 145 U. S. 156; 36 L. Ed. 658; 12 S. Ct. 825; McCormick v. Aultman, 169 U. S. 606; 42 L. Ed. 875; 18 S. Ct. 443. The authorities for the eleventh rule are McDowell v. Ideal, 187 Fed. 814; 109 C. C. A. 574; Moneyweight v. Toledo, 187 Fed. 826; 109 C. C. A. 586.

[1] The term "laches," as used in the law, probably comes from the *laxus* of the Roman law. It might be translated rather freely by the old New England term "shiftlessness." It is such neglect, delay, or disregard as will disentitle one to claim or maintain that which otherwise would have been his right.

8. The court will not review the decision of the Commissioner, unless manifest error appears on the record.

9. The specification may be modified the better to disclose the invention, but the invention must be the same.

10. If the patentee abandons his application for a reissue, he is entitled to the restoration of his original patent.

11. The present tendency is to enforce these rules with so great rigor that any enlargement of a claim is practically barred; and intervening rights will defeat any enlargement of the claim, no matter how the defect arose.

The moral to be pointed is evident. See to it that the original patent is properly solicited. Employ a competent attorney and follow up his work. Otherwise a valuable invention may fail of any protection, though patented.

§ 52. Foreign Patents

Under the old statute, if an invention had been patented previously in a foreign country to the applicant or his assigns, then the United States patent expired with the foreign patent first expiring. By amendment of the act the provision now is that the United States application must be filed within twelve months from the date of filing the first foreign application in the case of inventions included under § 4886 and within four months in the case of designs.[1]

The enactment of this amendment has resulted in the establishment of conventions between the United States and most foreign countries, so that the twelve-month provision and the four-month provision is mutual.[2]

It is unnecessary to consider this subject further, except to say a word regarding the advisability of procuring foreign patents. Of course, in the case of a broad, basic invention, one which is of large and general significance, foreign patents are advisable; but it is my observation that improvements and lesser inventions rarely repay the outlay. The reasons are evident. First, even with a domestic patent, it requires the presence and push of the owner to make it profitable; and this is

---

[1] R. S. § 4887.
[2] The principal countries in the convention union are Austria, Belgium, Denmark, France, Germany, Great Britain, Hungary, Italy, Norway, Portugal, Spain, Sweden, Switzerland, Mexico, Cuba, Brazil, Japan, Australasian Commonwealth, New Zealand.

quite as essential in other countries. Second, foreign investors rarely take kindly to an American invention unless it has been thoroughly developed at home. It is also to be noted that foreign taxes are large, and that one who takes out patents in foreign countries should be in financial position to push them and to pay the taxes which increase from year to year.

CHAPTER VII

CLAIM CONSTRUCTION

§ 53. General Statements

In this chapter is to be found a rather formidable undertaking, which finds its justification only in its importance to the engineer. It is an attempt to state under a few headings and by means of a few illustrations the main principles of claim construction — a subject which, in a general work on the law of patents, should occupy an entire volume. This attempt is made for the reason that the engineer has to deal with this phase of the subject of patents very frequently; and, generally, without help from others.

This might be illustrated in various ways, but a single, common occurrence will suffice. For the purpose of doing certain special work, the engineer wishes to design and build a machine generally similar to a standard patented machine, but having special changed or added features. May he do so? He has before him the patent covering the standard machine, which he reads, but the reading of which sheds little light. Neither his training as an engineer nor his experience with his patent attorney in the past seem to help him. Then why not take it to the patent attorney and let him settle it? For a very simple reason: The attorney can help him only after he has designed the new machine, so that it may be compared with the patent. In other words, in order to make use of his attorney, he must "go it blind," design his machine, and then very likely find that his gray matter and time have been wasted. The first and main purpose of this chapter is, therefore, to enable the engineer to mark the limits of the claims of a patent — the actual limits — before he starts designing or inventing, and then design or invent to a purpose.

Again, the engineer needs to understand generally the subject of claim construction in order to coöperate with his patent attorney; and also to read understandingly the reports and opinions of attorneys and experts regarding the scope and construction of claims.

In the third place, the engineer must be able

to deliver expert opinions on questions often running into the patent field, and he must be prepared to testify as an expert. And while it would be absurd to presume that these brief and fragmentary remarks could in any sense qualify him so to act, they are quite sufficient to convince any thoughtful person of the necessity of deeper study.

Logically, and from a textbook point of view, many of the subjects hereunder belong with the subject of infringement. The grouping here is for convenience. Utility is the first consideration in the making of this handbook.

§ 54. Statutory Provision

In dealing with the claim we are dealing with the vital organ of the patent. The surgeon may explore much of the human body with impunity, but when he nears the heart, he moves with caution. We may do much as we please with the specification; but when we come to the claim, a small incision may sever a vital connection, and the patent is dead. At the beginning, then, the statute should be before us.[1]

[1] R. S. 4888.

Before any inventor or discoverer shall receive a patent for his invention or discovery, he shall make application therefor, in writing, to the Commissioner of Patents, and shall file in the Patent Office a written description of the same, and of the manner and process of making, constructing, compounding, and using it, in such full, clear, concise, and exact terms as to enable any person skilled in the art or science to which it appertains, or with which it is most nearly connected, to make, construct, compound, and use the same; and in case of a machine, he shall explain the principle thereof, and the best mode in which he has contemplated applying that principle, so as to distinguish it from other inventions; and he shall particularly point out and distinctly claim the part, improvement, or combination which he claims as his invention or discovery. The specification and claim shall be signed by the inventor and attested by two witnesses.

And in construing a claim with reference to the prior art we should have before us the four negations of the pivotal section of the patent statute.[1]

1. Not known or used by others in this country before his invention or discovery thereof.

2. Not patented or described in any printed publication in this or any foreign country before

[1] R. S. 4886.

his invention or discovery thereof, or more than two years prior to his application.

3. Not in public use or on sale in this country for more than two years prior to his application.

4. Not abandoned.

§ 55. General Rules of Patent Construction

In the confines of a single case[1] Judge Putnam has given a dozen rules of general patent construction which should be in view before taking up the rules specially applicable to the claims.

1. The claims are to be construed in the light of the circumstances and in view of their different purposes.

2. The patent should be considered as a unit.

3. That instead of a literal construction which would render the patent frivolous and ineffectual, nonessentials should not be allowed to control.

4. That words, phrases or limitations positively introduced by the patentee leave no option, and must be followed.

5. That amendments, like amendments to a contract, have immediate bearing, and greater effect must be attached to them than would be

[1] Reece v. Globe, 61 Fed. 958; 10 C. C. A. 194.

given them if forming a part of the original application.

6. That the *ut res magis valeat quam pereat* should apply.

7. That a patent should be construed in a liberal spirit.

8. That the titles by which patents are held should not be overthrown on doubts or objections capable of solution.

9. That in construing the claim, the court will remember that the specification and claims are often unskillfully drawn.

10. That a claim will be construed, if possible, to sustain the patentee's right to all he has invented.

11. That this rule will not be carried to the extent of interpolating anything the patent does not contain.

12. That the application of the doctrine of equivalents should be just and reasonable.

§ 56. Plain Intent and Meaning

It is the rule that a claim will be construed according to its plain intent and meaning, and, while it will be construed favorably to the patentee, the courts will not strain the language either to save the claim, to find infringement, or to find anticipation.[1] It will be presumed that the inventor knew his invention, knew the art, and claimed what he invented.[2] While it will be found that the courts seem to differ as to the latitude and liberality of construction,[3] it will be observed also that these seeming differences are due in large measure to the character of the patents dealt with. For it must be remembered always that, whatever the rules may be, it is not in human nature to accord to an improved tin whistle the same consideration that is spontaneously evoked by a great invention. Courts must be just; but courts may be just and generous also when dealing with the product of a larger mind.

§ 57. Analysis of Claim

Going back to the drawings and main claim of the Selden patent under § 23, let us repeat the claim and the analysis of it.

---

[1] Mac. Pat. §§ 219, 222.
[2] *Ibid.*, § 244.
[3] *Ibid.*, §§ 245–247.

1. The combination with a road locomotive, provided with suitable running gear including a propelling wheel and steering mechanism, of a liquid hydrocarbon gas-engine of the compression type, comprising one or more power cylinders, a suitable liquid fuel receptacle, a power shaft connected with and arranged to run faster than the propelling wheel, an intermediate clutch or disconnecting device and a suitable carriage body adapted to the conveyance of persons or goods, substantially as described.

An analysis of this claim discloses the following elements:

1. Running gear,
2. Gas-engine of the compression type,
3. Fuel receptacle,
4. Power shaft,
5. Clutch,
6. Carriage body.

Here is a claim of six elements. It is that which Selden said was the essence of his invention. Is it perfectly plain? Undoubtedly so except as to the second element — a gas-engine of the compression type. There the experts disagreed; and the appellate court, in preventing this cold-storage patent from levying tribute upon the entire gas

CLAIM CONSTRUCTION [§ 57

ropelled automobile art, indulged in a line of reasoning which many of us are not able to follow.[1]

Now take the claim of the Collar Button Patent, under § 24. It reads:

A collar or sleeve button having a hollow bead and stem, the said head, stem and the base plate or back of said button being shaped and made of a single continuous piece of sheet metal, substantially as herein shown and described.

Analysis shows these elements or characteristics:
1. A hollow bead,
2. A hollow stem,
3. Head, stem and base plate a single piece.

Next take the Phenacetine claim under § 24:

The product herein described which has the following characteristics: It crystallizes in white leaves, melting at 135° centigrade; not coloring on addition of acids or alkalies; is little soluble in cold water; more so in hot water; easily soluble in alcohol, ether, chloroform, or benzole; is without taste; and has the general composition of $C_{10}H_{13}O_2N$.

Its characteristics are:
1. Crystallizes in white leaves,
2. Melts at 135° centigrade,

[1] Columbia v. Duerr, 184 Fed. 893; 107 C. C. A. 215.

[§ 57] ENGINEERS' HANDBOOK ON PATENTS

3. Does not color on adding acids or alkalies,
4. Little soluble in cold water,
5. More soluble in hot water,
6. Easily soluble in alcohol, ether, chloroform or benzole,
7. Has no taste,
8. Composition, $C_{10}H_{13}O_2N$.

Finally take the Mitchell patent — a patent covering a process which is a true chemical process. This patent which lay at the foundation of the great "Ivory Soap" industry, was twice considered by the Supreme Court, the first time held not to be infringed because improperly construed,[1] and the second time held valid and infringed.[2] The single claim reads:

The manufacturing of fat acids and glycerine from fatty bodies by the action of water at a high temperature and pressure.

It is evident that we cannot analyze this claim as we have done with the preceding.

We now have before us typical claims of the four classes of patentable subject-matter — a

---

[1] Mitchell v. Tilghman, 19 Wall. 287; 22 L. Ed. 125.
[2] Tilghman v. Proctor, 102 U. S. 707; 26 L. Ed. 279.

machine, an article of manufacture, a composition of matter, and a process. Certain aspects of each may now be considered.

There are six elements in the Selden claim, three elements or characteristics in the collar button claim, eight characteristics in the phenacetine claim, and merely the statement of a single step in the glycerine process claim. Does the rule applicable to combinations — that the fewer the elements the broader the claim — apply to all these classes?

It is clear that the combination rule cannot apply to the glycerine process claim, because that claim contains but a single step, unless we assume that there might be other processes for producing glycerine from fats which involved more than a single step. It would rarely, if ever, occur that one process could be differentiated from another by a mere count of steps. It is, therefore, safe to say that, while one might in some cases apply the combination rule to a process claim, it would be of doubtful value. The eight characteristics of the phenacetine claim are mere characteristics — not factors in the composition. The composition is either phenacetine or it is something else; it would be no more or no less phenacetine if identifiable by one or a dozen characteristics. Hence it is clear that the combination rule does not apply to a composition of matter. In the collar button claim, while the three characteristics are characteristics which identify the article, they are also *essential* characteristics which differentiate it as a species of its genus. Suppose that I were able to omit the first characteristic — a hollow bead — without using anything its equivalent: I would then change the species. Hence we may conclude that the combination rule applies to articles of manufacture where the characteristics are expressed in terms of essentials.

This discussion, in addition to showing the limits of the combination rule, should serve also to show that the problem of claim analysis is far from facile at all times. Even with combination claims it is common to find the elements qualified and limited, or expressed in terms which may or may not be qualifying or limiting. Nor is it possible to avoid these conditions; for an invention is, at its foundation, a mental act or vision, and any attempt to express, limit and delimit it must be more or less relative and vague.

§ 58. Combinations

Hundreds of pages of sayings wise or of doubtful wisdom have been written concerning combinations. But two quotations from the Supreme Court cover the subject completely for our needs. Justice Clifford said:[1]

In case of a claim for a combination, where all of the elements of the invention are old, and where the invention consists merely in the new combination of old elements or devices whereby a new and useful result is attained, such combination is sufficiently described if the elements or devices of which it is composed are all named and their mode of operation given, and the new and useful result to be accomplished pointed out, so that those skilled in the art and the public may know the extent and nature of the claims, and what the parts are which coöperate to produce the described new and useful result.

And Justice Blatchford said:[2]

The claims of the patents sued on in this case are claims for combinations. In such claims, if the patentee specifies any element as entering

---

[1] Bates v. Coe, 98 U. S. 31; 25 L. Ed. 68.
[2] Fay v. Cordesman, 109 U. S. 408; 27 L. Ed. 979; 3 S. Ct. 236.

into the combination either directly by the language of the claim or by such a reference to the descriptive part of the specification as carries such element into the claim, he makes such element material to the combination and the court cannot declare it to be immaterial. It is his province to make his own claim and his privilege to restrict it. If it be a claim to a combination, and be restricted to specified elements, all must be regarded as material, leaving open only the question, whether an omitted part is supplied by an equivalent device or instrumentality.

§ 59. Reference to Specifications and Drawings

Compare two statements. Justice Strong said:[1]

Claims must be limited to the means described in the specification.

Justice McKenna said:[2]

The description does not necessarily limit the claims.

One or the other of these statements is good law; both cannot be. They are 35 years apart, and the statement of Justice McKenna shows in some

---

[1] Hailes *v.* VanWormer, 87 U. S. 353; 22 L. Ed. 247.
[2] Continental *v.* Eastern, 210 U. S. 405; 51 L. Ed. 1122; 28 S. Ct. 748.

measure the progress of those years. To those who have the habit of Lot's wife, and can see good only in the past, such a comparison must be disquieting.

Three propositions as to the use of the specifications and drawings in construing the claims are beyond controversy:[1]

1. We may refer to them to explain the claim.

2. We may refer to them to determine the limits of the claim.

3. We may never refer to them to expand the claim.

§ 60. Beneficial Uses

In construing a claim, particularly with reference to a use differing in some degree from that contemplated by the patentee, it must be borne in mind that the patentee is entitled to the beneficial uses to which his invention may be put, whether he contemplated those uses or not.[2] The function or use is not the thing patented. The patentee may be ignorant or the solicitor may have bungled; but if the thing is disclosed and claimed, we may

---

[1] Mac. Pat. §§ 212, 224, 900.

[2] Goshen v. Bissell, 72 Fed. 67; 19 C. C. A. 13, and cases there cited.

not belittle the claim by reason of such shortcomings or by reason of industrial development since the invention was made.

But we shall see, in considering the subject of equivalents (§ 62), that a generic invention is accorded a much wider range than a specific improvement; so that, in a sense, beneficial uses will be attributed to the one in far larger degree than to the other.

§ 61. Generic Inventions and Specific Improvements

As just said, a generic patent is given a wider range of equivalents. If we bear in mind that the classification of patents as generic and specific is more or less arbitrary; that as matter of fact patents range all the way from the basic discovery that is distinctly pioneer to the narrow and microscopic affair more often encountered — if we bear these facts in mind the following statement by Judge Coxe [1] is to the point:

Limitations upon the claims by which the defendant seeks to avoid infringement proceed

---

[1] Electric v. Pittsburg, 125 Fed. 926; 60 C. C. A. 636.

upon the initial fallacy that in a generic process patent, every phenomenon observed during the operation and every minute detail described must be read into the claims and that the least departure from the claims as so construed avoids infringement. The position is not tenable. In a patent like Bradley's (one of the basic patents in the process for electrolytic reduction of aluminum) the claims should be as broad as the invention and, even if unnecessary and unreasonable limitations are incorporated in the claims, the court should interpret them liberally and not permit a defendant to escape who reaches the same result by analogous means, although he may employ additional elements and improved mechanical appliances.

With narrow, small improvements, each improver will be limited to his own small field, and no more.[1] But there are inventions distinctly improvements and seemingly narrow, which perform a function never performed before, or never performed successfully, which at once meet an extensive demand and achieve large commercial success. Such inventions attain something approaching primary rank, and the claims should be liberally construed.[2]

[1] Cochrane v. Deener, 94 U. S. 780; 24 L. Ed. 139.
[2] Chicago v. Miller, 133 Fed. 541; 66 C. C. A. 517.

§ 62. Equivalents

An equivalent, in the law of patents, is defined to be "any act or substance which is known in the arts as a proper substitute for some other art or substance, employed already as an element in an invention, whose substitution for that other act or substance does not in any manner vary the idea of means. It possesses three characteristics: (1) It must be capable of performing the same office in the invention as the act or substance whose place it supplies; (2) it must relate to the form of embodiment alone, and not affect in any degree the idea of means; (3) it must have been known in the arts at the date of the patent, as endowed with this capacity."[1]

Devices in one machine may be called by the same name as those contained in another, and yet they may be quite unlike in the sense of the patent law, in a case where those in one of the machines perform different functions from those in the other. In determining about similarities and differences, courts of justice are not governed merely by the names of things; but they look at the machines and their devices in the light of what they do or what office or function they perform, and how they perform it, and find that a thing is substantially the same as another, if it performs substantially the same function or office

[1] Duff v. Forgie, 59 Fed. 772; 8 C. C. A. 261.

in substantially the same way to obtain substantially the same result, and that devices are substantially different when they perform different duties in a substantially different way, or produce a substantially different result.[1]

Equivalents may be claimed by a patentee of an invention consisting of a combination of old elements or ingredients, as well as of any other valid patented improvement, provided the arrangement of parts comprising the invention is new, and will produce a new and useful result. Such a patentee may doubtless invoke the doctrine of equivalents as against an infringer of the patent; but the term "equivalent" as applied to such an invention, is special in its signification, and somewhat different from what is meant when the term is applied to an invention consisting of a new device or an entirely new machine.[2]

These three quotations well-nigh cover the subject. Two further quotations will complete the statement of law.

When an invention is one of a primary character, and the mechanical functions performed by the machine are, as a whole, entirely new, all subsequent machines which employ substantially the same means to accomplish the same result are infringements, although the subsequent machine

[1] Bates v. Coe, 98 U. S. 31; 25 L. Ed. 68.
[2] Imhauser v. Buerk, 101 U. S. 647; 25 L. Ed. 945.

may contain improvements in the separate mechanisms which go to make up the machine.¹

It is manifest, therefore, that it was not meant to decide that only pioneer patents are entitled to invoke the doctrine of equivalents, but that it was decided that the range of equivalents depends upon and varies with the degree of invention.²

Such is the law; but how shall we determine the facts? This is the difficult part. The problem is generally complex. Engineers and experts will differ as to what is and what is not an equivalent. I recall an instance where counsel had been badgering my witness until he became nettled, and made answer something like this: " Yes, sir, theoretically this cam-action is the equivalent of that threaded sleeve and lever. Yes, sir, a buzz-saw is the equivalent of a cross-cut saw, and a cross-cut saw is the equivalent of a hand-saw, and a hand-saw is the equivalent of a wood-rasp, and a wood-rasp is the equivalent of a three-cornered file; but if you will take a cord of four-foot hard maple and cut it up with a three-

---

[1] Morley v. Lancaster, 129 U. S. 263; 32 L. Ed. 715; 9 S. Ct. 299.

[2] Continental v. Eastern, 210 U. S. 405; 51 L. Ed. 1122; 28 S. Ct. 748.

cornered file, I guess you will modify your ideas of equivalents."

One ingredient, too often lacking in patent law and elsewhere, which resolves such problems as this subject presents, is common sense. Academic reasoning and the citing of many cases generally fails to arrive. At no point in the law of patents is that rare quality more in demand than in dealing with the subject of equivalents.

§ 63. Dissecting Claims

It is evident that a claim may not be expanded beyond its proper content. No rule is better settled. And a rule which should be equally well settled is that forbidding dissection of a claim for the purpose of anticipation piecemeal. Take the Selden claim, for example: The elements could have been found, all of them singly and some of them in combination. By such a course the examiner could have shown in one patent a running gear with steering mechanism and a carriage body; in another a gas-engine with a power shaft and a fuel receptacle; in a third a clutch in connection with a shaft; and then he could have stated in the dogmatic style of the office that it did not require invention to combine these.

This is the familiar, common practice of the Patent Office. That it is wrong is self-evident; that it cannot be stopped so long as we have the present type of examiner is also evident to those who have had long experience with the Patent Office.

But it is otherwise with the courts. They will not permit dissecting and anticipation piecemeal.[1] A claim is an entirety and must be so treated.

§ 64. Limitation of Claim

There are numerous conditions which limit the scope of a claim. It is not possible to do more than note briefly the main instances which so operate.

¶ 1. *The Prior Art*

The prior art necessarily includes all prior patents and publications, both domestic and foreign, and all domestic use prior to the actual date of invention. It may be said that the only difference between limitation by the prior art

---

[1] Mac. Pat. §§ 67, 68, 87, 89, 91, 693.

and anticipation is that the former maims the claim while the latter kills it. And it not infrequently is the fact that the maiming is so serious that the claim is to all intents and purposes dead. For example, the claim of the Selden patent was not held void, but it was construed so narrowly in view of the prior art that it had no power to reach any of the alleged infringers. The court held that the second element — a gas-engine of the compression type — was limited to an engine of the Brayton type, and did not include an engine of the Otto type.[1] Since all automobile engines in practical use are of the Otto type, the court might as well have said that the claim was void so far as leaving any life in it was concerned. This, to my mind, is reduction to absurdity; for thus limited the claim fails to cover an operative, useful device. It therefore lacks the second requirement of the statute — utility.

The general rule in this matter is:[2]

The extent of novelty which can be read into a claim must be limited by the state of the art.

---

[1] Columbia *v.* Duerr, 184 Fed. 893; 107 C. C. A. 215.
[2] Consolidated *v.* Walker, 138 U. S. 124; 34 L. Ed. 920; 11 S. Ct. 292.

How shall the engineer find what the state of the art is? There are several courses. If the investigation is to be thorough and complete, the matter should be referred to the patent attorney with instructions to make a scope and validity search. This he will do by having a competent searcher secure a copy of the file wrapper contents of the application of the patent and go through the entire art and allied arts, domestic and foreign. This differs little from a complete infringement search. A second course is to procure copies of the patents that were cited against the application as it went through the Patent Office. This may or may not be conclusive of the facts sought. Often it is sufficient. If it is found not to be, then a scope and validity examination should follow. A third method, and one coming into practice with large concerns, is to have complete files of the subclasses of domestic patents relating to the art or arts in which the concern is engaged. Properly classified, catalogued and cross referenced, such a file is useful in a very large degree. It was once my task to procure, classify, cross reference and card catalogue some six thousand patents for one client. The cost was large, but it proved a wise expenditure even before the work was entirely completed by saving the company from investing a sum greater than the entire cost — in a patent tested by the prior art and found worthless.

¶ 2. *By Terms of Application*

When the patentee specifies a particular form as a means by which the effect of his invention is produced or otherwise confines himself to a particular form of what he describes, he is limited thereby in his claim for infringement.[1]

Look for a limitation of this kind in a patent solicited by a no-patent-no-pay advertiser. To illustrate: An application came into my hands after it had been filed by one of these advertising concerns and several claims allowed. The application covered a certain type of engine in which the cylinders were secured to a bedplate by a peculiar flange. This flange was both peculiar and distinctive, but was wholly unnecessary to the invention. The solicitors had illustrated and described it minutely as a feature of the invention, and either made it a direct element of the claims

---

[1] Green *v.* Buckley, 135 Fed. 540; 68 C. C. A. 70.

or made it so by implication. The claims, therefore, covered nothing but this flange. Omit the flange and use the kind found on any engine and there could be no claim for infringement. It took a year to get out of this limitation and secure proper claims.

So important is this subject that another illustration may be permitted. The owner of the supposed basic patent upon a clutch in extensive and general use came to me to bring suit against a number of large users. Upon examination of the patent it was found that the solicitors, whose names have been before the public by advertisement for years, had made an insignificant and negligible feature of the device the main feature in the specification, and not a single claim of the patent could be read without the inbringing of that feature as an essential element. The inventor saved a few dollars in securing his patent and lost a fortune by so doing.

¶ 3. *By Patent Office Action*

If an applicant, in order to get his patent, accepts one with a narrower claim than that contained in his original application, he is bound by it.¹ And having once narrowed the claim to secure it, he may not claim that it should be construed as it might have been if not amended, whether the narrowing was justifiable or not.²

Such limitations are distinctly disclaimers; but it does not follow by any means that any amendment to a claim upon reference to the prior art narrows the claim and operates as a disclaimer.³ The rule is this: If the amendment to the claim is made to *avoid* a prior patent, then there is limitation; if it is made to *distinguish* the claim from the prior art, and no more, it is not limitation. No single question of construction has been the subject of so much judicial ruling as this.⁴

¶ 4. *By Reference Characters*

Suppose that Selden had drawn his claim to read thus:

'The combination with a road locomotive provided with suitable running gear, including a

---

¹ Shepard *v.* Carrigan, 116 U. S. 593; 29 L. Ed. 723; 6 S. Ct. 493.
² Roemer *v.* Peddie, 132 U. S. 313; 33 L. Ed. 382; 10 S. Ct. 98.
³ Hillborn *v.* Hale, 69 Fed. 958; 16 C. C. A. 569.
⁴ Mac. Pat. §§ 207, 208.

propelling wheel B, and steering mechanism G, a liquid hydrocarbon gas-engine of the compression type L, a suitable liquid fuel receptacle U, a power shaft Q, a clutch Y, and a carriage body A.'

Under the early rules of construction, these reference characters would have limited the claim to the precise devices shown. This rule was properly reversed so that the law now is: [1]

If the invention is of a pioneer character, highly meritorious in conception and usefulness, the mere use of letters has been held not to limit the inventor to the exact form of the device shown, but he is entitled to a broader conception of his patent, in view of the advance he has made in the art. However, if the field of invention is limited, and an improvement of narrow character has been made, just sufficient to cross the line which divides mechanical improvement from patentable invention, the inventor will be allowed the specific description shown and no more.

¶ 5. *By Words of Limitation*

Claims will be found ending with "substantially as described," "substantially as and for the pur-

[1] Hendy *v.* Golden, 127 U. S. 370; 32 L. Ed. 207; 8 S. Ct. 1275.

poses set forth," and like phrases. This practice, however, is becoming obsolete. The rule regarding the effect of such terms is substantially identical with that stated above regarding reference characters. If the patent is generic, they will be construed as implying breadth; if specific, the reverse.

¶ 6. *Omitting Element — Unclaimed Element*

When the claim omits an element essential thereto, the same cannot be read into it by implication.[1] Such omission may leave the claim wholly inoperative and useless; and this condition often arises through the attorney drawing the claim attempting to broaden the claim by reducing the number of elements to the minimum, with the result that he draws a claim covering less than an operative combination.

The cure for such omission — if there is not another claim properly covering the combination — must be, if at all, by surrender and reissue. I say, if at all; for since errors in judgment on the part of a solicitor are not matters of inadvertence,

---

[1] Western *v.* Ansonia, 114 U. S. 447; 29 L. Ed. 210; 5 S. Ct. 447.

accident, or mistake of which the patentee may take advantage,[1] it would seem that such error may be fatal.

Of course, actual failure to claim limits the patent.

¶ 7. *By Disclaimer or Reissue*

It matters not whether the disclaimer was a part of the original application, inserted by amendment, or made subsequent to the issue of the patent. In either case it is a part of the patent; and that which has been once disclaimed cannot be recalled. In like manner, a reissue may, either by actual narrowing of the claim because more had been claimed than was permissible, or by broadening a claim so that it is actually invalid, have the effect of limitation.

§ 65. Construction with Reference to Anticipation

This section, strictly speaking, deals with problems of anticipation. It is included here because the construction of the claim must always be in view of the prior art (§ 64, ¶ 1), and because the determination of anticipation or nonanticipation

---

[1] Moneyweight *v.* Toledo, 187 Fed. 826; 109 C. C. A. 586.

always involves the twofold act of construction of the claim in question and interpretation of the prior art.

¶ 1. *Ex Post Facto Judgment*

And this subject must begin with a stern warning. It is always easy, after a thing has been done, to say that it is so simple, so obvious, so plain, so easy, that any ordinary mechanic could have done it. After Glidden had produced his barbed wire fence (see cut under § 34, ¶ 5), it was seemingly no more than a clever trick performable by any one having some wire and a pair of pliers to twist the barb D around a wire a and then twist a wire z and the wire a together to clamp the barb. It was easy to move the core out of contact with the diaphragm — a mere fraction of an inch — to make the Bell telephone. As the Supreme Court said in another case:[1]

It should be borne in mind that this process was not one accidentally discovered, but was the result of a long search for the very purpose. The surprise is that the manufacturers of steel, having

[1] Carnegie v. Cambria, 185 U. S. 403; 46 L. Ed. 968; 22 S. Ct. 698; see also Mac. Pat. § 693.

felt the want for so many years, should have never discovered from the multiplicity of patents and of processes introduced into this suit, and well known to the manufacturers of steel, that it was but a step from what they already knew to that which they had spent years in endeavoring to find out. It only remains now for the wisdom which comes after the fact to teach us that Jones (the inventor) discovered nothing, invented nothing, accomplished nothing.

¶ 2. *Prior Public Use*

Our sense of humor sometimes saves us. The refinement of prior public use established in the Second Circuit,[1] in a coffin case, where the court held that the testimony of a single witness, testifying from memory alone, was sufficient to defeat a patent, would indeed be melancholy could we not put beside it another coffin case — a case not reported, but believed to be authentic. In this coffin case the attorney for defendant was seeking to anticipate a claim on a coffin lid. He heard of such a lid having been invented by a man in the backwoods of Michigan. He went there only to find the man dead and buried in the coffin he had

---

[1] National *v.* Stolts, 157 Fed. 392; 85 C. C. A. 300.

invented, and the only coffin of the kind ever made. Having secured permission from relatives and graveyard authorities, he dug up the inventor, put him in another coffin and reburied him, took the coffin having the lid in question and, having proved the date of the funeral and burial and that it was a public funeral and burial, put the coffin into the case as an exhibit, duly identified, stood it up on end before the court, and defeated the claim of the patent in suit.

Of course the rule is that [1]

Oral testimony, unsupported by patents or exhibits, tending to show prior use of a device regularly patented is, in the nature of the case, open to grave suspicion.

But the "grave suspicion" evidently does not hold when we are dealing with a coffin patent. Lawyers will go to all extremes, witnesses will stretch the truth to the breaking point and beyond, and experts will indulge in reasoning which, anywhere else, would entitle them to quarters in an asylum.

It is here that the engineer should rise above

---

[1] Deering *v.* Winona, 155 U. S. 286; 39 L. Ed. 153; 15 S. Ct. 118.

such common conduct. He does not dare do an untruth in designing a machine; he does not dare stretch the truth when he is calculating strain or load; why should he do either in dealing with a question involving a patent?

The point is here: Stay by the facts as the evidence of prior use shows; stay by the plain meaning of the claim; stretch neither; compare them fairly, honestly, and take the consequences. No circumstance of business, no exigency of any situation, can justify any other course. To paraphrase: For what is an engineer profited if he shall gain a whole lawsuit and lose his own professional standing? or what shall an engineer give in exchange for his good name?

¶ 3. *Analogous or Nonanalogous Use*

This subject has been considered under § 29, ¶ 9, and what has just been said in the preceding paragraph applies. The rule of construction is this:[1]

Anticipation ought not to be found in prior devices in the art to which a patent belongs unless they are of such a character as to furnish clear, if

---

[1] Williams *v.* American, 86 Fed. 641; 30 C. C. A. 318.

not unmistakable suggestion, of the improvement in question; and if the anticipatory suggestion comes from another art, it should, of course, have less significance, proportioned inversely to the distance from which it is brought.

¶ 4. *Abandoned Device or Experiment*

The question here is, with what are you comparing the claim in question? Is it an abandoned device or an abandoned experiment — which? If an experiment, that ends it; for it had become nothing so long as it was purely an experiment. But if it was an abandoned device which had ceased to be an experiment, then it becomes a question of public use. Was there in such case, public use? A reading of the court decisions [1] will show that not infrequently the question of construction has been befogged through failure to distinguish between an abandoned device which may have passed the experimental stage and been in public use, as distinguished from a mere experiment which could not have so arrived.

[1] Mac. Pat. §§ 60, 61.

¶ 5. *Inoperative Device*

Here, again, it is a question of starting with the actual facts. Was the device inoperative? If so, and the device of the claim in question is operative, it is a fair presumption at least that there can be no anticipation.

An illustrative instance occurred in a case where the claim covered a combination in a stave-jointing machine in which the rotating knives were housed and the housing connected with a pipe so that the machine would act as a blower to carry away the shavings. A witness, with the patent in suit in his hand, testified minutely to a prior device which he said performed the same function by the same means. On cross-examination I relieved him of the copy of the patent in suit and made him restate the construction of the alleged anticipating machine in detail. The result was that he testified to a construction where it was impossible to house more than the upper half of the cutter head, and hence impossible to make the cutter head and housing act as a blower.

It frequently happens that one reads into a prior device characteristics which it does not possess, and which, once eliminated, leave the device inoperative so far as the function in question is concerned.

¶ 6. *Foreign Use*

In view of the plain statement of the statute,[1] comment on this subject seems unnecessary, for the statute says:

Whenever it appears that a patentee, at the time of making his application for a patent, believed himself to be the original and first inventor or discoverer of the thing patented, the same shall not be held to be void on account of the invention or discovery, or any part thereof, having been known or used in a foreign country, before his invention or discovery thereof, if it had not been patented or described in a printed publication.

But ignorance of this provision by many who should know of it justifies its quotation; and there is another justification. It may turn out that the foreign use may have become prior domestic use by importation; and of course such importation of a foreign-made device and its use makes it domestic use.[2] But merely because an American

---

[1] R. S. 4923.
[2] Stuart *v.* Auger, 149 Fed. 748; 79 C. C. A. 60.

traveling abroad has seen such prior use and returns with that knowledge in his head does not constitute anticipation.[1]

¶ 7. *Prior Domestic Patent*

This is too large a subject to more than touch upon. A half-dozen suggestions may prove useful; but it is to be remembered that these are so far from exhaustive that they can accomplish no more than put the investigator with face toward the subject.

1. Bear in mind that the comparison is not between the claim of the patent under consideration and the claim or claims of the prior patent; but between the claim in question and all that the prior patent fairly discloses, whether claimed or not.

2. That the fact that the prior patent has never gone into public use, but is a mere paper patent, is immaterial if the invention of the claim is present.[2]

3. Neither the dates of the patents nor dates of application are necessarily controlling as to priority of actual invention. (See § 19.)

---

[1] Acme *v.* Cary, 101 Fed. 269; 41 C. C. A. 338.
[2] Mac. Pat. §§ 92, 93.

4. That the fact of issuance of the later patent is some evidence of patentable difference.[1]

5. That the Patent Office practice of anticipation piecemeal will not hold with the courts. (See § 63.)

6. That when they may be applied, the eight tests of novelty under § 34 are useful in construing a claim.

A repetition of the remark concerning team work between engineer and attorney is in place here. Claim construction is a mixture, frequently, of engineering and law. The engineer cannot afford to infringe upon his profession by wasting his time learning details and case law which a question of this kind may involve. If the problem becomes complex, the attorney should be called in and team work should follow. One large manufacturing concern known to me has practiced such team work between its head engineers and its attorneys with the result that, with extensive litigation extending over a period of some twenty-five years, it has won every suit in which it has been involved.

¶ 8. *Prior Publication*

The date of publication must be proved to constitute anticipation.[2] And the publication

---

[1] Warren v. Casey, 93 Fed. 963; 36 C. C. A. 29.
[2] Elizabeth v. American, 97 U. S. 126; 24 L. Ed. 1000.

must disclose the invention in workable form, not requiring invention or extensive adaptation after the fact.[1]

Observation and experience suggest the following: It is rare that an anticipation in the form of a publication other than a patent is found clearly in point except in compositions of matter and processes. It must be borne in mind that France and Germany are in advance of us in chemistry and the allied branches of engineering; and that they publish without patenting much more extensively than we. The result is that it is not uncommon, upon filing a product or process application in Germany, to have cited some publication which clearly anticipates, and which the Patent Office at Washington entirely failed to discover. In fact, if one desires a composition of matter or a process tested out to the utmost as to its novelty, no better or more conclusive course can be taken than to file an application in Germany. The hostile attitude of the German government toward American enterprise will insure a most rigorous examination.

[1] Mac. Pat. §§ 105, 106.

¶ 9. *Prior Foreign Patent*

A single quotation covers this point. Judge Acheson, one of our great patent judges, said:[1]

It is a well settled and familiar doctrine that an invention patented here is not to be defeated by a prior foreign patent unless its descriptions or drawings contain or exhibit a substantial representation of the patented invention in such full, clear, and exact terms as to enable any person skilled in the art or science to which it appertains, without the necessity of making experiments, to practice the invention.

¶ 10. *Infringe-if-Later Test*

That which infringes if later would anticipate if earlier,[2] and vice versa. A test of this sort is effective where it can be applied readily; but the difficulty is that you rarely can apply this rule in one direction until you have proved its converse, and that, generally, is no easier than to reach an independent conclusion.

[1] Hanifen v. Godshalk, 84 Fed. 649; 28 C. C. A. 507.
[2] Knapp v. Morss, 150 U. S. 221; 37 L. Ed. 1059; 14 S. Ct. 81.

§ 66. Construction with Reference to Infringement

When there is charged or prospective infringement, nothing short of a thorough course of action is to be considered for a moment. Following any other course is to breed trouble; and yet this is exactly what many engineers and manufacturers do. Suppose your neighbor came to you and said, " I have just had a survey of my lot and find that your building is over the line on my premises." Do you simply reply, " Well, I have a deed of my lot and I will stand on that"? Not if you are a wise man. You immediately have a survey made with great care; and if you find you are trespassing, you move, or effect an adjustment of the matter with your neighbor. You do so, not, perhaps, because you love your neighbor, but because you dread trouble. Why not be as wise with a patent?

What follows in this section will be chiefly useful to the engineer in determining whether a serious problem exists. If it does, he will go much farther, taking it up with his attorney and stopping nothing short of a conclusion upon which he will stand four-square, or one which requires adjustment or settlement or change of construction or manufacture. I assert without fear of successful contradiction that such course pursued generally would reduce patent litigation at least a quarter.

¶ 1. *Combinations*

One of the most instructive statements concerning mechanical combinations is the following:[1]

It must be considered that a new combination, if it produces new and useful results, is patentable, although all the constituents of the combination were well known and in common use before the combinations were made. But the result must be a product of the combination, and not a mere aggregation of several results, each the complete product of one of the combined elements. Combined results are not necessarily a novel result, nor are they an old result obtained in a new and useful manner. Merely bringing old devices into juxtaposition, and there allowing each to work out its own effect without the production of something novel, is not invention. No one by bringing together several old devices without producing a new and useful result, the joint product of the elements of the combination and something more than an aggregate of old results, can acquire a right to prevent others from using the same devices,

---

[1] Hailes *v.* VanWormer, 87 U. S. 353; 22 L. Ed. 247.

either singly or in other combinations, or, even if a new and useful result is obtained, can prevent others from using some of the devices, omitting others, in combination.

With such general statement in mind and the rule as to equivalents stated under § 62, let us note the following four points stated in the language of the decisions:

1. Identity.

In order to constitute an infringement, the whole combination must be used, because he claims not the various parts but the whole combination together.[1]

Every element of the combination must be used as patented, or the entire result is changed, and the machine sought to be held as infringing is a different one.[2]

2. Old elements, new function.

Actual inventors of a combination of two or more ingredients, are entitled, though the ingredients are old, if they produce a new and useful result, to restrain others from using the same.[3]

3. Different Combination, same result.

Combinations effecting similar results by similar

---

[1] Case *v.* Brown, 69 U. S. 320; 17 L. Ed. 817.
[2] Jones *v.* Munger, 49 Fed. 61; 1 C. C. A. 158.
[3] Seymour *v.* Osborne, 78 U. S. 516; 20 L. Ed. 33.

means, but employing different precedent conditions, are not necessarily identical or equivalent.[1]

If the combination of a defendant shows a mode of operation substantially different from that of the complainant, infringement is avoided even though the result of the operation of each is the same.[2]

4. Added elements.

One who appropriates a new and valuable patented combination cannot escape infringement by uniting or operating those elements by means of appropriate mechanical devices which differ from those which are pointed out for that purpose, but which are not claimed in the patent.[3]

But, —

When several elements, no one of which is novel, are united in a combination which is the subject of a patent, and these several elements are thereafter united with another element into a new combination, and this new combination performs a work which the patented combination could not, there is no infringement.[4]

¶ 2. *Process*

The rules of construction as to process claims are believed not to differ in any material feature

---

[1] National *v.* Wheeler, 79 Fed. 432; 24 C. C. A. 663.
[2] Brammer *v.* Witte, 159 Fed. 726; 86 C. C. A. 207.
[3] Brammer *v.* Schroeder, 106 Fed. 918; 46 C. C. A. 41.
[4] U. S. *v.* Berdan, 156 U. S. 552; 39 L. Ed. 530; 15 S. Ct. 420.

from those applicable to combinations, except that in processes and compositions the distinctions and differences are more subtle and require in large measure the assistance of the expert. There is an old rule which would seem to make the rule of equivalents much more generous in compositions and processes,[1] but it is believed that the later rulings have put this class of invention on an equal footing with machines.[2]

¶ 3. *Valeat quam Pereat Rule*

There is an ancient rule which Judge Putnam approves (see § 55), which amounts to this: If, in order to make out infringement, you have to construe a claim so broadly that it would be anticipated as so construed, this should not be done, because it is better to let the claim live in its narrow bounds than to kill it by subjecting it to any strain.

In any aspect, in my opinion, it is a foolish rule. If the claim does not cover the alleged infringement and is not generic so that it may have a reasonable range of equivalency, then it cannot

---

[1] Tyler v. Boston, 74 U. S. 327; 19 L. Ed. 93.
[2] Mac. Pat. §§ 816–821.

be so broadened at all, and there is an end of the matter. If it must be so narrowed that it is emasculated, it should go to the cemetery of dead monopolies.

¶ 4. *Repairing and Rebuilding*

The question frequently confronts the engineer as to how far he may go in repairing or rebuilding a patented machine without committing infringement. While the sale of a patented article carries with it the right to make ordinary repairs, there is no right given to rebuild or make repairs which amount to rebuilding.[1]

The points to be considered are these: What is the scope of the claim and what features of the machine does it cover? Has the use or accident destroyed the thing that is the combination of the claim so that the combination has ceased to exist? Will the rebuilding be a re-creation of the combination of the claim? While it is not possible to lay down a rule which will cover all circumstances and conditions, viewed in the light suggested the question differs little, if any, from that of determining what would or would not be infringement in

---

[1] Mac. Pat. §§ 523, 524.

building any machine some features of which are patented.

§ 67. The Province of the Expert

To see ourselves as others see us, let us begin this subject with three quotations from the courts.

Experts may be examined to explain terms of art, and the state of the art at any given time. They may explain to the court and jury the machines, models or drawings exhibited. They may point out the difference or identity of the mechanical devices involved in their construction. The maxim of *cuique in suo arte credendum* permits them to be examined to questions of art or science peculiar to their trade or profession; but professors or mechanics cannot be received to prove to the court or jury what is the proper or legal construction of any instrument of writing. A judge may obtain information from them, if he desire it, on matters which he does not clearly comprehend, but cannot be compelled to receive their opinions as matter of evidence.[1]

The testimony of a capable and conscientious expert, in a case which admits of his employment, cannot but be at once helpful to the court and creditable to the witness; but it is a sorry situation for the display either of skill or candor when, not to hurt the cause he was employed to promote,

[1] Winans *v.* N. Y. & Erie, 21 How. 88; 16 L. Ed. 68.

the expert must suppress his opinions upon all matters of controlling significance, and restrict his testimony to the pointing out of superficial and obvious distinctions of structural forms that involve no conceivable differences of function or operation, — a task of mere drudgery, which a common mechanic, accustomed to work by lines laid down for him by another, could perform quite as well.[1]

Frequently an expert witness may be of much aid to the court in explaining matters which can only be appreciated and understood by learning higher than the ordinary; but his province is to instruct and not to decide; and even the instruction is of uncertain value when it is colored from standing in the place of the partisan for one of the parties. Usually the testimony of one competent witness on each side is enough to insure a full and fair elucidation of what is recondite in the case. The voice of a single teacher is worth more than a confusion of many tongues.[2]

Perhaps it would be well to rest the subject upon these statements of the courts, but the evils of expert evidence in patent causes have grown so gross that a special word to the engineer, out of my own experience and observation, is in place.

It is not the degree one holds, nor yet the

---

[1] Chuse v. Ide, 89 Fed. 491; 32 C. C. A. 260.
[2] American v. Cleveland, 158 Fed. 978; 86 C. C. A. 182.

place one has attained in the industrial world, that gives weight to the evidence of an expert. In a noted case one expert was called by both sides; there was evidence of character. Another case might be cited where an expert of large experience testified in two cases involving the same patent, in the one making out a strong case for the patent and in the other an equally strong case against it. It was a state judge who said that "there were three degrees of experts, — positive, comparative and superlative: liars, damn liars, and just experts." It is the sad fact that experts have won such distinctions. While patent experts have not attained to the superlative as have the alienists in murder trials, they have won an unenviable reputation.

It is time for a change, and it is time that the engineer should refuse to prostitute his reputation and standing by becoming a partisan and advocate in patent causes. There is no need of it; and the remedy is simple. Let the engineer simply decline to so lend his ability and learning. He may lose a stray fee, but he will gain in the end; and above all that, he will have saved and safeguarded his reputation.

CHAPTER VIII

INFRINGEMENT

§ 68. General Statement and the Statute

WHILE the subject of infringement, as it stands related to the engineer, has been covered in large measure by the preceding chapter, there are further considerations which make a short chapter on the subject necessary.

The statute gives to the patentee and his assigns an absolute monopoly coextensive with the dominion of the Federal Government for seventeen years from the date of his patent to make, use, and sell his invention;[1] and it gives him the right to go into the United States courts and sue for redress. Such is the position and right of the owner of a patent. As will be seen later, his right to sue for infringement includes the right to recover damages or profits and also to secure through injunction the prevention of further invasion of his rights.[2] Without these his patent

---

[1] R. S. 4884.
[2] *Ibid.*, 4919, 4920, 4921.

would be a useless piece of paper. It is necessary, therefore, to consider the act of infringement in some of its familiar aspects.

§ 69. Who may Commit Infringement?

Infringement is an act in violation of a Federal statute which may be committed by any person, firm, or corporation, without respect to age, sex, domicile, or place of incorporation. While an infant under years of discretion, an idiot, or an insane person might perhaps be excused for an infringing act upon the ground of lack of mental responsibility, such an exigency is most improbable. It is sufficiently near the truth for our purposes to say that any person may commit infringement. There are, however, circumstances which excuse acts which otherwise might be infringement, and four of these will be first considered.

¶ 1. *Joint Owners*

Unless the terms of assignment making two or more persons joint owners specifies otherwise, there can be no infringement between them. They are tenants in common, and each has full and free use of the patent.¹ This may be avoided, to some extent at least, as we shall see when we come to consider the subject under assignments (§§ 86–89).

¶ 2. *Licensor and Licensee*

As between a licensor holding title to the patent or a part thereof and a licensee holding an ordinary right to enjoy the patent, there can be no infringement. But if the licensee is, in reality, the sole owner of the patent by reason of the license being exclusive, for the entire patent right and the entire life of the patent, then, as in the case of a former owner, a licensor may infringe.² And, of course, a licensee may violate the terms and limits of his assignment and become an infringer.

¶ 3. *Copartners*

Copartners cannot infringe each other under a patent owned or licensed in common;³ but if one copartner, acting in the interests of the firm, infringes a patent owned by a person not a member

---

[1] McDuffee *v.* Hestonville, 162 Fed. 36; 89 C. C. A. 76.
[2] Waterman *v.* Shipman, 55 Fed. 982; 5 C. C. A. 371.
[3] Wade *v.* Metcalf, 129 U. S. 202; 32 L. Ed. 661; 9 S. Ct. 271.

of the firm, he not only makes himself liable but all of his copartners.

¶ 4. *Assignor and Assignee*

And it follows that, as between assignor and assignee, there can be no infringement so long as each holds some interest in the patent. But when the assignor retains no interest, he may become an infringer, and what is more, he cannot contest the validity of the patent.[1]

¶ 5. *Corporations*

Not only may a corporation commit an infringement directly, but it may be liable as an infringer if it coöperates with a person or another corporation in committing such an act.[2]

The personal liability of an officer of a corporation for infringing acts committed by his corporation is regarded in various ways by the different circuits. Generally speaking, when the act of infringement arises in the ordinary course of corporate business he is not liable; but if he

---

[1] Woodward *v.* Boston, 60 Fed. 283; 8 C. C. A. 622.
[2] Railroad *v.* Winans, 58 U. S. 31; 15 L. Ed. 27.

has been the instigator and active agent, he may be personally liable, at least in some circuits.[1]

¶ 6. *Employer and Employee*

Of course, an ordinary workman making or using a thing for his employer would not be liable for infringement;[2] but at the same time, an injunction issued against an employer includes his servants, agents and employees, and if the employee had knowledge of the injunction, he might be guilty of contempt of court if he thus knowingly violated the order.

I know of no case where an engineer has been differentiated from other employees of a corporation and held personally liable by reason of his superior ability or because he may have designed or invented the infringing device; but I think this fact is to be noted: The tendency is to go through the shield of corporate existence and punish the individual wrongdoer. The arm of the law grows longer, and it may yet reach an officer or engineer who has been the moving and prime cause of a corporate wrong.

[1] Mac. Pat. § 481.
[2] Graham *v.* Earl, 92 Fed. 155; 34 C. C. A. 267.

Of course the law makes no distinction here between a private and a public corporation. A state, city, town, church, hospital, and even the Federal Government may come within the jurisdiction of the courts, although the Federal Government cannot be restrained by injunction, and must be sued in the Court of Claims.[1]

¶ 7. *Intent — Ignorance*

Neither nonintent nor ignorance can excuse. People are presumed to know both the law and the existing patents in their art.[2]

§ 70. As to the Nature of the Act

The statute gives the patentee the exclusive right to make, use, and sell, and the invasion of any one of these rights may be infringement. There is a common notion — no one ever knew where it originated — that one may make a patented thing for his own use without violation of the law. This idea was expressed to me by an engineer recently. Suppose every person might construct a wireless telegraph for his own use:

---

[1] Mac. Pat. §§ 428, 429.
[2] *Ibid.*, § 508.

where would the Marconi company be? To state the proposition answers it. A single making, using, or selling is enough. And we have seen (§ 66, ¶ 4) that even repairing or rebuilding a patented device may be infringement.

¶ 1. *Contributory Infringement*

Suppose I should make sheet metal and sell it to a person whom I knew was going to use it in making expanded metal by the process to which we have referred (§ 25) without right or license under the patent; would I be an infringer? Yes. Suppose I did not know it was to be used in committing an act of infringement: would I than be an infringer? No, because I would be merely making a standard article of general utility without any intent of becoming a party to an infringing act. Suppose I should make a part peculiar to a Marconi instrument and sell it to some one: would I infringe? Certainly. But suppose I did not know what use was to be made of it; surely I would not be guilty of a wrongful act. On the contrary, I surely would; for if I have enough intelligence to make such a device, I have enough intelligence to inquire what it is for and to be on my guard not to infringe a patent; and if my intelligence is so shy and lopsided that I know only what is convenient to know and am blissfully ignorant of that which is inconvenient to know, the law will not excuse me because I am conveniently idiotic.[1]

These are the plain, established rules of contributory infringement, and a little reflection is convincing of their justice. Were the law otherwise, the door would be opened for all sorts of evasion and trickery.

But there is another rule of contributory infringement, established long ago, but recently brought into discussion by the Dick Case.[2] This is the situation; The Dick company sells mimeographs with a printed license agreement attached permanently to each machine which says, in substance, that the machine is leased, not sold, under the express condition that the stencils, ink, etc., used upon the machine shall be purchased from the Dick company. The defendant in the Dick Case made a mimeograph ink and sold it, knowing it was to be used on a Dick machine. The

---

[1] Mac. Pat. §§ 474–478.
[2] Henry v. Dick, 224 U. S. 1; 56 L. Ed. 645; 32 S. Ct. 364.

Supreme Court held this to be contributory infringement. There are, and long have been, many cases so holding; but it is probable that, before long, this law will be materially modified, either by a reconsideration of the question by the Supreme Court or by the enactment of a statute. Hence the reader will be on his guard.

¶ 2. *Importation*

Suppose I had purchased in France an automobile embodying the combination of the Selden patent and brought the car to this country; would I escape infringement? By no means, because immediately I would be using the device of the patent in the United States. But suppose I had purchased a car from a French maker who held a license under a French patent granted to and owned by Selden, and had thus paid tribute to the Selden invention through the French maker; could I say to Selden, "I have purchased my car from your French licensee, paid him tribute which he has, in turn, paid to you. I therefore have the right to use my car when and where I please." The law says I may not so justify myself.[1]

[1] Mac. Pat. § 505.

¶ 3. *Territorial Rights*

But the rule is different with reference to territorial rights within the United States. Having had two coffin patents for illustration, let us have a third. Suppose you own a patent on a coffin lid and give a territorial right to an undertaker for the city of Boston and the county in which it is situated; and suppose I should die in Boston and the undertaker should put me in a coffin covered by the patent and then take me into a neighboring county, outside his territorial license, and bury me or have another undertaker do the job: would I, in my last, long sleep, be infringing? This is the exact situation which the Supreme Court said was not infringement.[1]

When one has regularly purchased an article made under a territorial license, unless there are special restrictions to which the purchaser consents or of which he has knowledge, he may use or sell it at will where he pleases.

¶ 4. *Buying a Machine Without the Right to Use*

While it is, of course, the general rule that a patented thing once lawfully made and sold

[1] Adams *v.* Burks, 84 U. S. 453; 21 L. Ed. 700.

carries the right to use and sell, there may be exceptions. It does not necessarily follow that the monopoly right goes with the right to the material thing. This is best illustrated by a case in hand. Smith, as patentee, gave a shop license to his company to use his inventions. His company went into bankruptcy, and the trustee proceeded to sell the property of the company. I insisted that the machines made under the shop license should be sold with notice that they were built and used under a shop license and that the purchaser could not buy the right to use them. That was prior to the decision of the Mimeograph Case,[1] and that case held my position sound. The purchaser of those machines, if the owner of the patents sees fit to enforce his rights, may use them for nothing better than junk.

§ 71. Infringement of the Different Classes of Patentable Invention

While what has been said concerning claim construction in Chapter VII applies generally and broadly at this point, there are certain peculiarities

[1] Henry v. Dick, 224 U. S. 1; 56 L. Ed. 645; 32 S. Ct. 364.

inherent in the various classes of patentable invention to be noted.

¶ 1. *Art or Process*

Since a process consists in certain steps, the question is one of identity or equivalency of step, and we cannot determine infringement by what the process produces.[1]

¶ 2. *A Machine*

This has been practically covered in the preceding chapter; but the difficulty generally encountered is lack of identity element by element, and, therefore, the difficulty of proving equivalency. The mere fact that the machine does the same thing as the machine of the patent proves nothing; it is establishment of identity or equivalency of elements of the combination claimed that is called for. Finding more than the specified elements of the combination may be immaterial — is immaterial so long as the combination is not destroyed — but less than the specified elements of the combination with no equivalent factor defeats the charge of infringement.

[1] Matheson *v.* Campbell, 78 Fed. 910; 24 C. C. A. 284.

¶ 3. *Machine and Manufacture*

Suppose there is a patent upon the machine and also a patent upon the manufacture the machine produces. If you buy the machine, you have the right to produce the article.[1] But suppose you acquire only the right to make, use, or sell the patented article — not the right to use the machine. Then you infringe if you use the machine.[2] Of course, if there is no patent upon the product or manufacture produced by a patented machine, the innocent purchaser of such product or manufacture is not an infringer even if the product is that of an infringing machine.[3]

¶ 4. *Manufacture or Composition of Matter*

The infringement of an article of manufacture is ordinarily evident on its face. But in the case of a composition of matter, if it is an obscure product such as a chemical derivation, the question becomes most difficult. In such case resort must

---

[1] Morgan *v.* Albany, 152 U. S. 425; 38 L. Ed. 500; 14 S. Ct. 627.

[2] Belknap *v.* Schild, 161 U. S. 10; 16 L. Ed. 599; 16 S. Ct. 443.

[3] Keplinger *v.* DeYoung, 10 Wheat. 358; 6 L. Ed. 341; Welsbach *v.* Union, 101 Fed. 131; 41 C. C. A. 255.

be had to the testimony of experts and the experiments which they make.[1] Even then experts will differ, and often cloud rather than clear the issue. A case within my own knowledge will illustrate. The suit was for the infringement of a process for making soap, and the defense was that the process of the patent would not make soap — in other words, if the steps of the process were followed, saponification would not take place. It was a quarrel of experts. Among the exhibits was soap made by the defendants, which they stoutly maintained was not made by the process of the patent, and also soap that had been made exactly according to the process of the patent. After the day of evidence-taking the exhibits were stored in a closet of the old building wherein I studied law. The building was infested by rats. Now, it is well known that rats will eat grease, but will not eat soap. In the morning the exhibits were brought out, and those made by the defendant were intact, while those made by the process of the patent were nibbled freely by the rats; and the rats — not the experts — had decided the case.

[1] Matheson *v.* Campbell, 78 Fed. 910; 24 C. C. A. 284.

¶ 5. *Improvements*

With an improvement the presumption is that the device or process or product is similar to the thing improved upon. Hence we must look mainly to the elements to discover infringement. The fact that the defendant is practicing his art under a subsequent patent may be evidence of patentable difference; but it in no wise implies that he may not be an infringer when his patent is a mere improvement. But when the improvement partakes of a wholly different nature, the fact that there is a prior patent performing the same function raises no presumption of infringement.[1]

¶ 6. *Designs*

Turn back to the statement of Judge Grosscup under § 27, and it will be seen that his excellent definition of a design is also an excellent statement of what must be the characteristics of infringement. It is a question of comparison, not of analysis; it is a question of identity of æsthetic impression. It is not a question of artistic or technical superiority, for the one may be more

---

[1] Mac. Pat. §§ 506, 507.

finely executed than the other without affecting the issue; it is a question of artistic likeness.

§ 72. Some General Observations

I believe the general trend of decision for the past decade has been to establish certain general rules with reference to infringement which may be thus summarized:

1. To give a generic invention its just due; and if the alleged act of infringement is an infraction of good business morals, to hold infringement if possible.

2. If the improvement is a vital one, to give it a liberal construction; but not such as will prevent legitimate advance by further improvement.

3. Where the patent is narrow and insignificant, to hold infringement only where the act is a Chinese copy.

4. To put the evidence of experts in the category of special briefs, rather than that of sworn evidence.

5. More and more, as the years pass, in cases of doubt, to make large utility and use a factor, not only in determining novelty, but also, where

applicable, in determining the question of infringement.

6. That ultimately the professional engineer rather than the professional expert, will have commanding weight with the courts.

CHAPTER IX

PATENT LITIGATION

§ 73. General View of the Subject

To state what the engineer wants to know, and to state it in language free from legal phraseology; to presume that he has some general knowledge of the law and its various workings, but not to presume too much; to make the treatment orderly and free from gaps and breaks where technical matters are omitted; to keep to a scientific habit, and yet not get dry as dust — these are some of the problems in writing this chapter.

Sherman said, "War is hell." It is true that, in the past, patent litigation had been industrial hell. But while this paragraph was being put in type, a great and wonderful event had taken place. On November 4, 1912, the Supreme Court handed down a revision of the Equity Rules, to take effect February 1, 1913, which govern every Federal district and circuit court. No act of Congress, no court decision of recent years, is comparable in importance with this great event. It advances our system of equity practice and procedure from the age of Elizabeth to the front rank of twentieth century judicature. I repeat, it is an act of stupendous moment — an act which will be understood only as time proves that, by it, human rights have been advanced a century and more at a single step. Especially does this act of the Supreme Court raise patent litigation into a new and higher realm. It abolishes immeasurably the old delays, the old technicalities which gave undue advantage to unscrupulous wealth and power, and, in the main, the enormous expenses which made the inventor, the engineer and the manufacturer regard patent litigation not only as war but never-ending war. So that, for the first time in the history of our patent system, patent litigation has been put upon a common footing of practice and procedure of simplicity and efficiency with other legal differences.

But war is a necessary evil and will remain so until the human race has evolved much farther. Patent litigation will remain for a like period and for like reasons. The engineer must, when necessity demands, attack or defend; and he will also pursue the wise course of preparing for war in times of peace. If Lincoln and his cabinet had known the geography of war as Sherman knew it when he made his march to the sea — if Lincoln and those about him had known their geography, they would have forced McClellan out of his inaction on the James and hastened the end of the struggle. So, to know the geography of patent litigation will enable the engineer and his associates to force action and hasten the day of peace.

To follow the figure further, let us first note the main continental divisions of the subject. They are: (1) rights in unpatented inventions; (2) rights in the property of the patent; (3) rights arising with the grant. Against any one of these a wrong may be committed.

§ 74. Wrongs Against Unpatented Inventions

Until the patent issues there is no monopoly under which suit for infringement can be brought; but the patent statute provides for the protection of the inventor and also for the protection of the public. The statute, in the first place, provides a court in the Patent Office — although it is not termed a court — wherein an inventor may establish his right to a patent.[1] This is an interference proceeding, described briefly in § 46. Here the inventor may prosecute his claim to a patent as against another who has appropriated his invention and has secured, or is in process of securing, a patent. By proper procedure and presentation of the evidence in the case, he may invoke judicial ruling, first by the examiner of interferences, then by a series of appeals to the examiners-in-chief, to the Commissioner in person, to the Court of Appeals, D.C.; and finally, after he has exhausted all these, he may bring an action to compel the issue of a patent to him.[2] So that an inventor has abundant means for protecting his unpatented invention, if he is diligent; and when his patent is once issued, he may then prosecute trespassers as infringers.

On the other hand, the law will not permit an inventor to sleep on his rights or keep his invention unpatented, and finally use it as a trap to catch game. The statute first provides:[3]

Every person who purchases of the inventor or discoverer, or, with his knowledge and consent, constructs any newly invented or discovered

[1] R. S. 4903–4914.   [2] R. S. 4915.   [3] R. S. 4899.

machine, or other patentable article, prior to the application by the inventor or discoverer for a patent, or who sells or uses one so constructed, shall have the right to use, and vend to others to be used, the specific thing so made or purchased, without liability therefor.

And next it limits the inventor to two years of use before application and makes conduct amounting to abandonment fatal.[1] It also compels him to make oath of his inventorship,[2] and finally the courts have made diligence in reducing an invention to practice a further safeguard, as was seen under § 19. The statute further provides that an invention may be assigned and the assignment recorded in the Patent Office before the patent is granted.[3]

Thus it should be evident that the inventor is abundantly protected in his unpatented invention, provided only that he is diligent.

A word should be said here regarding the practice sometimes followed of keeping a process or a machine secret, rather than to protect it by patent. The law is this:[4]

---

[1] R. S. 4886.
[2] R. S. 4892.
[3] R. S. 4895, 4898.
[4] Park *v.* Hartman, 153 Fed. 24; 82 C. C. A. 158.

One who makes or vends an article which is made by a secret process or private formula cannot appeal to the protection of any statute creating a monopoly in his product. He has no special property in either a trade secret or a private formula. The process or formula is valuable only so long as he keeps it secret. The public is free to discover it if it can by fair and honest means, and, when discovered, any one has the right to use it.

While there are instances where a secret process has been long kept, and while machines have been kept under lock and key with some success, it is the general rule that a process leaks out and that a machine secreted rather than patented ultimately becomes known. If the secreted feature of a process or product can be determined from an analysis of the product, any attempt to keep it secret must fail. Such secretion seems justifiable only under one of two conditions: (1) where, from some circumstance, patent protection cannot be had, (2) where the secret is not discoverable by any analysis of product and is of such a character that the secrecy is readily maintained. And even in these circumstances there is always the probability that, in time, another will invent or discover the same thing.

§ 75. Wrongs Affecting Property Rights in Inventions

A patent is property, and as such it is given the same protection as any chattel. It has all the protection of a piece of personalty, and somewhat more, for the title or interest may be protected by recording in the Patent Office.

But questions relating to property rights in inventions and patents have nothing to do with infringement; a wrong against the property right being a wrong against property which may be redressed in any court having jurisdiction of such matters. A wrong against the monopoly is quite another thing, and of this the United States courts have exclusive jurisdiction.

The subject of property rights in patents comes up more fully in Chapter X, §§ 81–92.

§ 76. Wrongs Against Patented Inventions

These are acts of infringement, and are justiceable exclusively in the United States courts.[1] Let us have before us the three sections of the statutes which provide specially for infringement suits:[2]

---

[1] Judicial Code, Secs. 24, 256.
[2] R. S. 4919, 4920, 4921.

Damages for the infringement of any patent may be recovered by action on the case, in the name of the party interested either as patentee, assignee, or grantee. And whenever in any such action a verdict is rendered for the plaintiff, the court may enter judgment thereon for any sum above the amount found by the verdict as the actual damages sustained, according to the circumstances of the case, not exceeding three times the amount of such verdict, together with the costs.

In any action for infringement the defendant may plead the general issue, and, having given notice in writing to the plaintiff or his attorney thirty days before, may prove on trial any one or more of the following special matters:

First. That for the purpose of deceiving the public the description and specification filed by the patentee in the Patent Office was made to contain less than the whole truth relative to his invention or discovery, or more than is necessary to produce the desired effect; or,

Second. That he had surreptitiously or unjustly obtained the patent for that which was in fact invented by another, who was using reasonable diligence in adapting and perfecting the same; or,

Third. That it had been patented or described in some printed publication prior to his supposed invention or discovery thereof, or more than two years prior to his application for a patent therefor; or,

Fourth. That he was not the original and first inventor or discoverer of any material or substantial part of the thing patented; or,

Fifth. That it had been in public use or on sale in this country for more than two years before his application for a patent, or had been abandoned to the public.

And in notices as to proof of the previous invention, knowledge, or use of the thing patented, the defendant shall state the names of the patentees and the dates of their patents, and when granted, and the names and residences of the persons alleged to have invented or to have had the prior knowledge of the thing patented, and where and by whom it had been used; and if any one or more of the special matters alleged shall be found for the defendant, judgment shall be rendered for him with costs. And the like defenses may be pleaded in any suit in equity for relief against an alleged infringement; and proofs of the same may be given upon like notice in the answer of the defendant, and with the like effect.

The several courts vested with jurisdiction of cases arising under the patent laws shall have power to grant injunctions according to the course and principles of courts of equity, to prevent the violation of any right secured by patent, on such terms as the court may deem reasonable; and upon a decree being rendered in any such case for an infringement, the complainant shall be entitled to recover, in addition to the profits to be accounted for by the defendant, the damages the complainant has sustained thereby; and the court shall assess the same or cause the same to be assessed under its direction. And the court shall have the same power to increase such damages, in its discretion, as is given to increase the damages found by verdicts in actions in the nature of actions of trespass upon the case.

But in any suit or action brought for the infringement of any patent there shall be no recovery of profits or damages for any infringement committed more than six years before the filing of the bill of complaint or the issuing of the writ in such suit or action, and this provision shall apply to existing causes of action.

Sec. 2. That said courts when sitting in equity for the trial of patent causes, may impanel a jury of not less than five and not more than twelve persons, subject to such general rules in the premises as may, from time to time, be made by the Supreme Court, and submit to them such questions of fact arising in such cause as such circuit (now district) court shall deem expedient.

And the verdict of such jury shall be treated and proceeded upon in the same manner and with the same effect as in the case of issues sent from chancery to a court of law and returned with such findings.

It will be noted that these sections provide for actions at law and actions in equity. Since I am addressing these pages to engineers and not to lawyers, the distinction between an action at law and an action in equity should be indicated. It is sufficient for our purposes to say that an action at law demands the payment of damages—money. An action in equity asks the court to compel some action — either that the defendant shall do something, refrain from doing something, or account for something he has done; in other words, when you sue an infringer at law, you can do no more than get judgment that your patent is valid, that the defendant has infringed, and the award of a specific sum as damages for the infringement; while in equity you get a decree which holds your patent valid, infringed, an injunction restraining the defendant from further infringement, and an order for an accounting by the defendant where you may compel him to show and disgorge the profits he has made by the infringement. And the statute quoted above provides also that you may prove and recover damages in equity and that the damages so found may be increased to not more than threefold the actual damages found. But a reading of the cases will show any one that the courts are most reluctant in penalizing an infringer except in a most aggravated case.

Naturally, actions at law in patent causes are rare. It is only where the patent has expired, so that no equitable relief can be had, that a law action is justifiable. Hence the discussion will be confined mainly to equity actions.

§ 77. The Geography of an Equity Action

Let us follow an action in equity from Sumter to Appomattox. And let us do so for this reason: Much of the delay in patent suits is due to inaction on the part of attorneys — either from intent to wear down an adversary, from procrastination, from pressure of work, or from unadulterated laziness. Far from all of the delay so notorious in the past was due to our ancient and ineffective system of procedure, and the new Equity Rules — vigorous and effective as they are — cannot eliminate entirely unnecessary delay and expense. But if the engineer knows such to be the facts and knows something of the geography of the battle field, he may do much toward speeding the cause and winning or being beaten — either of which is preferable to a never-ending struggle.

The complainant files his bill of complaint with the clerk of the district court of the district in which the defendant resides or has an established place of business where infringement has been committed. The clerk issues a process called a subpœna which the marshal serves upon the defendant or his agents, which process requires the defendant to appear and answer within 20 days after the service of such subpœna. Under the old practice the defendant had at least 20 days within which to "appear," and at least 30 days more within which to answer or otherwise plead. And under the old rules it was at this point that the defendant could, instead of answering and for the purpose of delay, interpose dilatory pleadings, such as demurrer, special plea and exception. By the new rules all forms of technical pleadings are abolished, and the case is at issue (*i.e.*, ready for putting on the court calendar for trial) as soon as the answer is filed. Thus the new rules make a saving of time at this stage ranging from months to years.

At any time between the filing of the complaint and final decree by the court, the complainant may move for a preliminary injunction — that is, an injunction restraining the defendant from further infringement during the time the case is being tried out. This proceeding is given special consideration under § 79.

After the pleadings are in and the case is at issue, the taking of proofs begins — that is to say: (1) the complainant proves those things necessary to enable the court to find infringement, to issue a perpetual injunction, and a decree for an accounting of profits; (2) the defendant proves all things he is able to defeat the charge of infringement; (3) the complainant then puts in his answering evidence to those proofs of the defendant; (4) finally the defendant "rebuts" by answering as best he may the proofs last made.

And here is the most important and far-reaching change of the new Equity Rules. Under the old rules the proofs were seldom, if ever, taken in open court, but before notaries public at the various places where witnesses might reside or be found. This was the curse of the old system. Each side had three months within which to take proofs, and might tramp from Maine to Mexico doing so.

Moreover, the court not infrequently extended the time, so that the testimony-taking period might be drawn out into years. One suit in which I was counsel involved taking testimony in Troy, Detroit, Chicago, and Los Angeles — each a separate trip with Buffalo as a starting-point; and this is far from an extreme instance.

It was during this period that the piling up of expert testimony was indulged in beyond all reason. The record in the Selden case filled 32 large octavo volumes — a year's reading, if the court ever read it, which, of course, the court never did.

This record was then printed and put before the court; and then came preparation and printing of extensive briefs, and then the first argument of the case before a court. It took a week to argue the Selden case, but that is by no means the record.

Under the new Equity Rules all of the evidence, except in special instances where a witness cannot be brought before the court and in case of expert evidence (referred to presently), is taken in open court before a judge who rules upon the evidence and conducts the case much the same as in the trial of any other matter. When the evidence is in, the case is summed up and briefs filed.

The evidence is not typewritten and then printed at the enormous expense formerly required; and thus a patent case which formerly dragged on for months and years and ran into hundreds and thousands of dollars of expense may now be concluded in short time and at small cost.

Under § 72 I said I believed the tendency has been

To put the evidence of experts in the category of special briefs, rather than that of sworn evidence.

This was written before the new Equity Rules were handed down. The following is new Equity Rule 48:

In a case involving the validity or scope of a patent or trade-mark, the district court may, upon petition, order that the testimony in chief of expert witnesses, whose testimony is directed to matters of opinion, be set forth in affidavits filed as follows: Those of the plaintiff within forty days after the cause is at issue; those of the defendant within twenty days after plaintiff's time has expired; and rebutting affidavits within fifteen days after the expiration of the time for filing original affidavits. Should the opposite party desire the production of any affiant for cross-examination, the court or judge shall, on motion, direct that said cross-examination and any reëxamination take place before the court upon the trial, and unless the affiant is produced and submits to cross-examination in compliance with such direction, his affidavit shall not be used as evidence in the case.

This does not prove me a prophet, but it shows that I had read the minds of the courts aright. Under this rule this sort of evidence, which consumed nine-tenths of the time and caused nine-tenths of the expense, is now limited to seventy-five days from the time a case is at issue. Thus it is possible to complete the trial of a patent cause within little more than three months from the time suit is brought.

With the handing down of decision by the district judge a decree is entered dismissing the complaint if the defendant succeeds, and, if the complainant succeeds, ordering a perpetual injunction against future infringement and ordering an accounting of damages and profits. This accounting takes place before a master in chancery appointed by the court. He is given the power to bring before him both witnesses, books, and records from the examination of which he may ascertain the facts upon which to report to the court the profits the defendant has made by his infringing act and the losses or damages the complainant has sustained thereby. By the new rules this accounting is expedited, and the master is given greater powers to compel a defendant to disclose the facts.

Upon the coming in of this report arguments for and against it are heard by the district judge, who then confirms or modifies it as the law and the facts may require.

The old method of appeal by printing all of the evidence and all the immaterial rubbish that has been injected into the record is abolished. The defeated party may appeal to the circuit court of appeals by preparing a simple, condensed record of the evidence which shall be approved of by the district judge. And here is to be noted a change hardly less important than any heretofore noted. The old practice was, when an error in law or fact was made by the trial court, to reverse the case and send it back to be tried over again. New Equity Rule 46 provides:

When evidence is offered and excluded, and the party against whom the ruling is made excepts thereto at the time, the court shall take and report so much thereof, or make such a statement respecting it, as will clearly show the character of the evidence, the form in which it was offered, the objection made, the ruling, and the exception. If the appellate court shall be of opinion that the evidence should have been admitted, it shall not reverse the decree unless it be clearly of opinion that material prejudice will result from an affirmance, in which event it shall direct such further steps as justice may require.

Thus within the confines of a twenty-five page pamphlet the Supreme Court has taken our century-old system of equity practice, modernized it, simplified it, and removed the greatest stigma upon our system of judicature. The sting of patent litigation was delay; and the power was the ancient and inequitable rules of the Supreme Court. While patent litigation, like all other litigation, should be avoided if possible, it no longer presents the terrors of old, and is no more formidable or forbidding than any other legal controversy; and the patentee and the manufacturer may now look upon Justice as a friend who will speed his cause and protect his rights.

§ 78. Defenses in an Action for Infringement

While the preparation of defenses in an infringement suit is a matter for the attorney in the main, the engineer should know, in a general way, what conditions or proofs will enable him to defeat such a claim, and, conversely, what conditions or proofs will defeat his patent. As has been seen from the statute quoted in the preceding section,[1] five special defenses are specified, any one of which properly proved will defeat a charge of infringement. There are, in addition to these, a number of general defenses, which will be mentioned briefly following the five statutory defenses.

¶ 1. *Fraud or Misrepresentation in the Specification*

The statute says:

First. That for the purpose of deceiving the public the description and specification filed by the patentee in the Patent Office was made to contain less than the whole truth relative to his invention or discovery, or more than is necessary to produce the desired effect.

This defense is based on fraud. It is so rare that it may be practically disregarded; and there is

[1] R. S. 4920.

much doubt if it has any practical force in view of the decisions of the courts.[1]

¶ 2. *Fraud or Unfairness Against Another Inventor*

The statute says:

Second. That he had surreptitiously or unjustly obtained the patent for that which was in fact invented by another, who was using reasonable diligence in adapting and perfecting the same.

Suppose that you invent a machine which takes time and experiment to reduce it to working form, and suppose that I get the idea from you, appropriate it, get into the Patent Office and get my patent ahead of you and bring suit against you while you are diligently perfecting your invention. Prove that I have so done and my action fails. But this is a most improbable condition; for such condition in itself would in almost every case raise an interference.

¶ 3. *Anticipation*

The statute says:

Third. That it has been patented or described in some printed publication prior to his supposed invention or discovery thereof, or more than two years prior to his application for a patent therefor.

---

[1] Mac. Pat. § 317.

This is the defense of want of novelty, and is the defense raised ten to one over all the rest. It must be pleaded in strict conformity with the statute, and the proofs must conform in like manner. Bear in mind that this defense must antedate the invention — not merely the date of the patent or the date of filing of application.[1] Remember also that you cannot anticipate by a mere showing of the prior art; there is all the difference in the world between limiting the scope of a claim by the prior art and defeating a claim by proving anticipation.[2] You may limit a claim so that you escape infringement by a prior art showing. This is quite sufficient generally; and the courts are much more given to limiting a claim and finding noninfringement than they are to declaring a claim void.

¶ 4. *Noninventorship*

The statute says:

Fourth. That he was not the original and first inventor or discoverer of any material and substantial part of the thing patented.

---

[1] Walk. Pat., 3d Ed., § 447.
[2] Railroad v. Dubois, 79 U. S. 47; 20 L. Ed. 265.

I agree with Mr. Walker that this is but a subdivision, in a sense, of the preceding defense; and still it is designed to meet a different state of facts. Proofs under the third defense are largely documentary; under this defense they are likely to be quite otherwise; for if the thing is old, has never been patented, never described in a printed publication, the proofs are likely to be largely oral evidence; and in this connection the wise admonition of Justice Brown must be remembered:[1]

Oral evidence of anticipation must be regarded with grave doubt. The burden of proof rests upon the defendant, and every reasonable doubt should be resolved against him.

This does not mean, however, that such a defense cannot be made successfully,[2] but when your proofs are hazy or out of harmony, the court is against you.[3]

¶ 5. *Public Use or Abandonment*

Of these two defenses the statute says:

Fifth. That it had been in public use or on sale in this country for more than two years

---

[1] Barbed Wire Case, 143 U. S. 275; 36 L. Ed. 154; 12 S. Ct. 443.   [2] American *v.* Weston, 59 Fed. 47; 8 C. C. A 56.
[3] Untermeyer *v.* Freund, 58 Fed. 205; 7 C. C. A. 183.

before his application for a patent, or had been abandoned to the public.

These two defenses contrast rather than compare. The statute is absolute as to public use.[1] The two-year limit is the dead line. Neither the intent of the patentee, nor his condition, nor any other matter, can extend the period. On the other hand, abandonment is largely a question of intent, which may take place within the two-year limit before application, or between application and issue; and after the patent issues there may be such gross neglect of such unimpeachable character as to amount to abandonment.

In this connection it is proper to add a word of advice in view of a comparatively recent decision.[2] It is the practice of many manufacturers to put an invention in use and delay making patent application with the idea that they will improve upon and perfect it, and thus suit their convenience and also prolong the life of the patent. This is always dangerous, and the courts have recently held that if the invention is, in its essence, perfected, mere delay to improve and perfect it beyond the two-year limit actually defeats the patent.

[1] R. S. 4886.   [2] Star v. Crescent, 179 Fed. 856; 103 C. C. A. 342.

The proper course is to diligently perfect the invention, and when perfected, apply for the patent.

¶ 6. *Nonpatentability*

This is equivalent to saying that the thing patented does not come within any of the patentable classes which the statute names. It is a rare defense. I do not recall a case in which it was made a substantial issue.

¶ 7. *Noninvention*

This is the defense that the invention was nothing more than the exercise of mechanical skill. It is usually made a subsidiary, or secondary, defense.

¶ 8. *Joint Invention Patented to a Sole Applicant, or a Sole Invention Patented to Joint Applicants*

While the statute makes no mention of the subject of joint invention, the courts from the earliest times have recognized the right of joint inventors to receive a joint patent. In like manner, the courts have uniformly held that a joint invention cannot be patented upon the application of one inventor; nor can two persons, however interested in the invention as a piece of property, make joint application upon that ground.[1]

This subject presents interesting problems. I do not believe that one in ten of the patents issued to joint inventors are joint inventions at all. For example, the courts have held that an invention which consisted in the single thought that an incandescent lamp mantle could be coated with paraffin to give it strength for handling and shipment could not be a joint invention.[2] I think the test is this: If the invention is a single thought — a single idea — it is a sole invention; if it is composite — the association of several ideas — it may be joint.

¶ 9. *License — Release — Estoppel*

There are certain conditions which, if proved to exist, serve to excuse a defendant, even though he is infringing the patent. Chief among these are license, release and estoppel. It is evident that if one holds a license to enjoy the patent, he does not infringe. For example, if you employ a person

---

[1] Mac. Pat. § 704.
[2] Welsbach *v.* Cosmopolitan, 104 Fed. 83; 43 C. C. A. 418.

to improve and perfect your machine, and after having done so, he secures a patent upon those improvements he has made and brings suit against you, you have a perfect defense by way of license; for the fact of such employment and service gives you a shop right. And suppose again that this same person so improving your machine builds into it the combination which he has patented previously to such employment. Having done so, he has released his right so far as that machine is concerned, and cannot recall it. An estoppel is a condition where the defendant, by reason of some previous act or transaction, has precluded himself from the right to claim infringement. These need not be considered further, since they are questions of law which the attorney should settle.

¶ 10. *Defense of Not Guilty*

This is the defense of noninfringement. It is a defense alone and by itself, and it is also one which is secondary to and consequent upon some other defense. For example, if you set up as a defense prior public use, then noninfringement follows the proof of that defense, because if the claim is invalid there is no infringement. This defense is almost invariably pleaded.

¶ 11. *Other Defenses*

There are numerous other defenses which may be availed of at times, such as insufficiency of description, claims indistinct, claim not warranted by the application or the specification as it appears in the patent, failure to disclaim, double patenting, nonutility, repeal of patent, expiration of patent, failure to mark patented, statute of limitations, laches, want of title, and nonjurisdiction. It is enough to know that they exist.

A word of caution is needful here. We are prone to set up and attempt to prove too many defenses. Experience teaches that, generally speaking, a patent suit turns upon a single, pivotal issue. The proper course is to determine where the pivot is and, instead of wasting energy and confusing the defense, direct every force to act upon this single pivot. Only great lawyers have the courage to take this course at all times; but as one goes through the cases tried by great men he finds singleness of issue one of the characteristics. A multiplicity of defenses, especially if some of them are weak, serve to confuse the court and to suggest the fact that there is no single, strong defense.

§ 79. Preliminary Injunctions

With the increasing complexity of the subject-matter of invention and with the evils of delay in reaching a final decree where a perpetual injunction may issue, the remedy of a restraining order which prevents further infringement during the course and trial of the case becomes of first importance. Damages and profits rarely reimburse the owner of a patent for the mischief which infringement creates;[1] for infringement diverts or interferes with trade, disestablishes fixed prices, and often discredits an enterprise by the making of an inferior article. Where a preliminary injunction may be had, it is the most effective remedy in the law; for it stops invasion of the monopoly and also serves to make the infringer industrious in speeding the end of litigation.

This subject is replete with problems of the law which may not be considered here. But two things will be attempted: (1) to show what general conditions are prerequisite to the granting

[1] Allington *v.* Booth, 78 Fed. 878; 24 C. C. A. 378.

of a preliminary injunction and what general conditions will preclude such a grant, and (2) to show the special province of the engineer and his power at this critical moment.

And first of all it is to be noted that there is no *right* to a preliminary injunction. It is a privilege wholly within the discretion of the court.[1] And it therefore follows that a clear showing must be made and that the reasoning of expert, engineer and counsel must be sound and logical.

There are four essentials to the granting of an injunction pending suit: (1) clear title to the patent, (2) infringement reasonably clear and certain, (3) absence of delay in bringing suit and applying for the order, (4) a substantial moving cause in addition to these three.

1. It is self-evident that no court will grant this extraordinary relief when there is doubt whether the complainant owns the patent,[2] or where there is an open question whether the defendant may have some sort of license which would justify his acts.[3]

2. It must be reasonably clear that a condition

---

[1] Bissell *v.* Goshen, 72 Fed. 545; 19 C. C. A. 25.
[2] Armat *v.* Edison, 125 Fed. 939; 60 C. C. A. 380.
[3] American *v.* Talking Mach. 98 Fed. 729; 39 C. C. A. 249.

of actual infringement exists,[1] but this does not imply that an empy and loud-sounding protest of the defendant avails. It often happens that an expert makes an overstrained attempt here, either by sophistic distinctions or unwarrantable claim construction.

3. Diligence is a positive demand upon one who asks a court to exercise the prerogatives of equity. One may not sit idly and permit infringement, only to ask this relief at his convenience. Upon this the court will be both firm and lenient — firm in holding to inexcusable delay and lenient in recognizing valid excuses.[2]

4. In addition to these there must be a substantial moving cause. Among the various moving causes may be mentioned prior adjudication and establishment of the patent, long acquiescence by the public in its validity, unconscionable conduct on the part of the defendant and irreparable injury which would follow refusal to grant such relief.

On the other hand, in addition to the failure of any one of the first three essentials, counter-

---

[1] Menasha v. Dodge, 85 Fed. 971; 29 C. C. A. 508.
[2] Mac. Pat. §§ 558, 568.

vailing conditions may be shown by the defendant which will prevent the court from granting summary relief. Judge Coxe has summed up these in a general way as follows:[1]

1. The five patents in suit relate to a difficult, complex and abstruse subject. Because of its complicated character, the court should have the benefit of the opinions of those skilled in the art tested and clarified by cross-examination.

2. The patents have never been adjudicated or judicially construed.

3. The defendants assert that the patents are invalid for lack of novelty and invention and that the claims of three of the patents are not infringed.

4. We think the complainants have failed to prove a case of acquiescence. There has been no long continued public acquiescence.

5. We are not convinced that the complainants will suffer irreparable damage. That the defendants are amply responsible is conceded.

6. We think the record presents too many elements of doubt to warrant the issuing of a preliminary injunction.

The evidence which is brought before the court for and against a motion for a preliminary injunction consists chiefly of affidavits dealing with

[1] Hall *v.* General, 153 Fed. 907; 82 C. C. A. 653.

the facts, the patent in suit and the prior art. Each side presents its own affidavits and arguments, and it is here that the patent expert and the engineer have at once great opportunity for effective service and also for inexcusable failure. There are two reasons why the evidence of the expert and engineer carries more weight than that of the layman. The first is because he is skilled in his art, and this is the lesser reason. The second is because he is a man of science and holds the truth above all partisan considerations. This is the greater reason, but, alas, the one little regarded by many. These facts once fully grasped should leave little more to be said, but the failure of engineer and expert to live up to these facts justifies more. The engineer asked to prepare an affidavit for the court on motion for preliminary injunction, or asked to testify as an expert in a patent cause at any stage, should, first of all, reserve the right to refuse to testify until he has examined the matter judicially, and should flatly refuse unless he finds full justification for so doing. Here is the danger point. A retainer accepted without such reservation may place him where he feels under obligation to go on thin ice and in the end damage the cause and his own reputation. He does no kindness to his client in testifying under such circumstances; for no one makes a labored argument or a weak analysis without its being evident sooner or later.

But suppose he finds full justification in the case; how shall he proceed in preparing an affidavit for the court in an injunction proceeding? Shall he, therefore, plunge into an argument of the case? That is for the attorney. Shall he decide the issue upon his own showing? That is for the court, and the court will not brook trespass upon its province in this respect; the court may not call attention to such breach of province, but the witness who so does cancels his influence as an expert at once. On the other hand, there are two points to be constantly in mind: First, the court wants light — all the light it can get. Hence analysis is the first consideration. The analysis of the patent, the infringement and the prior art should be absolutely clear. Second, logical marshaling of the facts in such manner that no other conclusion is adducible than the one desired; and leave the drawing of that conclusion to the court.

§ 80. Damages and Profits

The choice here lies between a paragraph and a long chapter. The rules, measures, distinctions and refinements are too numerous for this short treatise; and, moreover, they are largely questions of law concerning which the engineer cares not a fig. His time is, or should be, too valuable to deal with such things which concern him little. The most that he wishes to know is the fact he has already gleaned from a reading of these pages — that both damages and profits are recoverable for an infringement, and that there are methods of ascertaining the amounts and assessing them against and collecting them from an infringer. Until a short time ago the law had been such that it was practically impossible to recover substantial damages or profits in the great majority of infringements — in cases where the entire profit to the defendant does not inhere in the patented feature; but with the recent decision of the Supreme Court in the Transformer Case,[1] it is both possible and practicable to prove and recover substantial damages or profits. Beyond these bald facts we need not go.

[1] Westinghouse *v.* Wagner, 225 U. S. 604; — L. Ed. —; 32 S. Ct. 691.

CHAPTER X

PROPERTY RIGHTS

§ 81. Introductory

In this last chapter we arrive at a subject which concerns the engineer vitally and perhaps more frequently than any other in the patent law. I shall take this opportunity to offer some general suggestions and observations which may be of more or less value. Most of us have seen a very small kitten — almost as soon as its eyes are open — bristle up and spit at a dog. This, they tell us, is traditional instinct. There is something of this traditional instinct between inventors and manufacturers. The inventor suspects that the manufacturer will do or defeat him if possible. The manufacturer expects to find in the inventor something of the slyness and treachery of a cat. Both have substantial ground for this traditional instinct. Time out of mind and times without number the inventor has been exploited and plundered out of a life labor. I have in my possession some of the long since expired patents of a man whose genius laid the foundation of a great industry. The president of that industry stole those inventions, tired out and wore down the inventor by interferences; and the old man — old before his time — died of privations in a shanty within sight of the great factory grown rich on the product of his brain. The only consolation — if such it be — is the fact that the president of that vast industry was also perishing from hunger and pain at the same time; for a cancer had fastened itself upon the vitals of him who refused even a crust to the man whom he had robbed. On the other hand, an instance might be cited where an inventor of large reputation came to me with the brazen proposition that I should draw a contract in a form which would enable him to do a manufacturer out of a large sum of money which he was investing in the inventor's patent.

There is this traditional instinct, and the honors are, I think, about even. We hear of the inventor who has been wronged, but the manufacturer is apt to take his medicine and say nothing. The manufacturer, however, has the advantage in that he has business ability; for while the inventor has imagination that enables him to invent and see only the rainbow, the manufacturer has that type of imagination that sees the pot of gold at the foot of the rainbow — and he gets it.

But what has this to do with property rights in patents? Recall two statements made at the outset: The old-time inventor is passing and the engineer is taking his place. A patent creates nothing. Add to these the further fact that the actual application of rules of property rights is with reference to the future in large measure, and it will be seen that the human equation is a very large factor. A patent is not a tangible thing that may be dealt with like a piece of land or a horse; it is a special, limited monopoly which secures certain rights and advantages. I know of no phase of the law wherein lies so large temptation to overreach — no condition wherein the lawyer is so often put to it to make men deal fairly and squarely.

§ 82. The Three States or Conditions

We may take the thing that lies beneath the grant and consider it in its three states or conditions with reference to the property rights which may inhere. In a sense we may liken this to the protection which the law gives to the person. There is, first, the protection given to the unborn child; second, that given the infant before it can assert its own rights; third, the grown man who must take care of himself. Such treatment gives us three conditions: (1) Future inventions; (2) Unpatented inventions; (3) Patented inventions. This classification is not in all respects scientific, but it is convenient.

§ 83. Future Inventions

The patent statute in no way recognizes a future invention. Not until it exists in such form that it may be made the subject of an application will the Patent Office recognize it in any manner.

And it is evident that a man may not sell or license or mortgage the whole future output of his brain. Such an assignment or contract would not be enforceable because, among other things, it would be too vague and indefinite for a court to enforce.[1] And a court will not pry into a man's

[1] Dalzell v. Dueber, 149 U. S. 315; 37 L. Ed. 749; 13 S. Ct. 886.

mind to discover an unknown or possible future invention.[1]

But the courts have always upheld assignments of future inventions where they are properly limited.[2] Observe how important this is. Suppose that you are manufacturing and an inventor comes to you with a valuable invention adapted to your needs. You see that, if you can secure absolute monopoly of the invention and all improvements, you can afford to pay a good sum for it; but you also see that it may be materially improved. It will not do to allow the inventor to go free, else he may, by a series of improvements, balk you in your business and render your purchased patent practically useless.[3] And, on the other hand, such a rule is as beneficial to the inventor as to the manufacturer; for were it otherwise, there would be little market for patents under such conditions.

Again, suppose that you are employed to use your engineering skill to perfect the machinery and processes of a factory, and that you invent

---

[1] Reece v. Fenwick, 140 Fed. 287; 72 C. C. A. 39.

[2] Troy v. Corning, 14 How. 193; 14 L. Ed. 383; Littlefield v. Perry, 88 U. S. 205; 22 L. Ed. 577.

[3] Reece v. Fenwick, 140 Fed. 287; 72 C. C. A. 39.

new machines and processes. Surely your employer cannot afford to give you the freedom and facilities of his factory only to have you go away and take out patents on the improvements you have made with his facilities and under pay from him, and sell or license them to some competitor. The law clearly sanctions an agreement so affecting future inventions, whether made during such employment or otherwise, if the agreement so specifies.[1] Furthermore, a court of equity will compel men to behave decently in such circumstances whether there is a specific agreement or not.[2]

Engineers are frequently called upon at the time of their employment to sign an agreement binding them to turn over all inventions they may make during the term of employment, and sometimes, for a period following the term of employment. With proper considerations therefor, there is not serious objection to such course, although it is to be noted that experience teaches that such a mortgage on one's brain is sometimes galling

---

[1] American v. Pungs, 141 Fed. 923; 73 C. C. A. 157; Regan v. Pacific, 49 Fed. 68; 1 C. C. A. 169.

[2] Nat. Wire Bound Box v. Healy, 189 Fed. 49; 110 C. C. A. 613.

— especially if it extends beyond the term of actual employment. In no case should an engineer mortgage a part of his brain indefinitely, even if the law would permit such course; yet it is but fair that an employer should have some reasonable protection in such conditions.

To sum up: While one may not agree to assign the entire future output of his brain, the law favors assignments of future inventions when specifically related to some art, and specifically limited as to time; that the courts will enforce such agreements, and will also, in some measure at least, compel men to play fair if no agreement exists.

§ 84. Unpatented Inventions

The right in an unpatented invention is primarily the right to mature it into a patent; and the statute impliedly recognizes this as a subsisting right in making an assignment of it recordable as soon as application is filed.[1] When the assignment is filed before issue the patent issues to the assignee, or if the interest be less than the whole, the patent discloses such interest. And an assignment of such an unpatented invention and all

[1] R. S. 4895.

improvements that may be made by the inventor will carry such improvements and be notice to the public.[1]

§ 85. Patented Inventions

When the patent issues, a physical character is established which places it substantially on a common footing with other forms of personal property. The property thus given specific form becomes subject to the control of courts having jurisdiction of other personalty; and from the date of the patent the United States district courts acquire jurisdiction of all matters of infringement. But purely as personal property, all matters of assignment, contract, license and possession are within the powers of the ordinary state courts.

And when the patent issues a legal title is established; for at that time the patent is recorded in the Patent Office; and with such recording public notice begins. A previously executed but unrecorded assignment, if now recorded, will pass the legal title to the assignee.

A legal title or interest in a patent, as will be

[1] Mac. Pat. §§ 160–164.

more fully discussed under § 87, is either (1) the whole patent, or (2) an undivided share of the exclusive right, or (3) an exclusive territorial interest. Anything less than one of these is a mere license holding, and vests no title in the patent.

An equitable title, therefore, must be such as is capable of being converted into one of the three above stated. Such an equitable title or interest may be converted into a legal title or interest by a written assignment or by a court decree.

§ 86. The Three Divisions of Interest

There are three forms or conditions of division of the legal title to a patent which should be thoroughly understood.

¶ 1. *Common Tenancy*

This is the common form of division. Suppose that Bell had assigned to me a one ten-thousandth interest in his telephone patent. I would then have been a tenant in common with him. I could license any telephone manufacturer in the United States; I could license any company to use the telephones; I could license any foreign maker of telephones so that he could send foreign-made Bell telephones into the United States and sell them here; I could manufacture, use and sell telephones without restriction. The only thing I could not do would be to interfere with Bell in doing likewise. Bell could have no share in the license fees or royalties I might obtain; nor I in his. Let me state the following in italics: *An assignment of a part interest in a patent without restrictions destroys the monopoly.* When you sell a part interest in a patent, you destroy the monopoly. When you buy a part interest in a patent, you secure little more than a license under the patent. Substantially all you secure beyond a mere license is the right to further dissipate the monopoly and the right to sue for infringement by joining your co-tenants.

Hence, in buying or selling patents, observe the following:

1. Buy a part interest in a patent when you wish to get inside the monopoly.

2. Do not buy a part interest with any idea that you will be able to exercise any control over the monopoly.

3. Sell a part interest only when you care nothing about preserving your monopoly.

I have put much emphasis upon this subject, because it is the fact that engineers, inventors and manufacturers are generally ignorant of the facts; and, strange enough, lawyers of experience in general practice are frequently no better informed. Instances have come to my notice repeatedly where an owner thought he still retained control of the monopoly because he sold less than one half of his patent, and where purchasers have thought they were securing control by buying more than a half interest; and it is far from uncommon for a patentee to suppose that if he sells a part interest, he still has a share in all of the profits arising from the patent.

¶ 2. *Territorial Assignments or Grants*

We have seen from the old coffin lid case under § 70, ¶ 3, that all a territorial assignment gives is the exclusive right to make within a given territory, but not the exclusive right to use or sell. Articles legitimately made outside the territory may be taken into the territory and used or sold there. While a territorial grant, as just stated, does not secure the exclusive right to use or sell, it does, nevertheless, give the exclusive right to use a process; and this, undoubtedly, is the chief value of a territorial right.

It is out of this provision that grew the numerous "county right" swindles. An enterprising Yankee would take a patented washing-machine, or a patented pancake-turner, or a patented feeding-trough such as Noah used in the Ark, and sell county rights to every farmer who would buy a gold brick. Some states have statutes designed to protect the innocent against this sort of patent fraud; and many states have provisions requiring that promissory notes given for an interest in a patent must have the fact stated on the face of the note.

It is not wide of the truth to say that a territorial right is a plan to catch suckers. There may have been use for such a provision; but we have long since outgrown it. Industrially speaking, the entire domain of to-day is not as large as was Massachusetts when the patent statute was first written. The need for territorial division of a patent to facilitate its exploitation does not exist.

¶ 3. *Tenancy by the Entirety — Trust Holdings*

Tenancy by the entirety is where the holders of interests cannot sell without common consent and where each participates in the earnings and profits. Assignments may be so made if specifically stated. This makes it necessary for all to join in any assignment, lease or license, and makes accounting between the cotenants necessary. It has its distinct advantages and it has objections also. The advantages are that it preserves the monopoly and gives to each tenant his proper share of the gains; the disadvantages are that one cotenant may do all the work and have to share the profits with the others, and that such holders are apt to get into dispute or disagreement, and one holder may take such a reactionary position as to render any use of the patent next to impossible.

The modern practice of putting the title to patents into the hands of a trustee or a holding company for the benefit of the persons interested appears to be the coming method, even in dealing with a single patent of considerable value. Such holding company or trustee holds the patents under the terms specified in the trust, and licenses or leases as those terms provide. In such circumstances the patent does not become an asset of a concern manufacturing under it, and, therefore, is not liable to be sold as an asset of the concern if it goes on the rocks — as so often happens. The legal title is thus always intact, so that the trustee or holding company may sue for infringement. It is believed that, where this course is expedient, it is the most satisfactory.

§ 87. Assignments

An assignment may be verbal or in writing; but, of course, only the latter passes the legal title.[1] The Supreme Court has defined clearly the difference between the assignment of an interest in a patent and a mere license in these terms:[2]

The monopoly thus granted is one entire thing, and cannot be divided into parts, except as authorized by those laws. The patentee or his asigns may, by instrument in writing, assign, grant and convey, either

---

[1] Dalzell v. Dueber, 149 U. S. 315; 37 L. Ed. 749; 13 S. Ct. 886.

[2] Waterman v. Mackenzie, 138 U. S. 252; 34 L. Ed. 923; 11 S. Ct. 334.

(1) The whole patent, comprising the exclusive right to make, use and vend the invention throughout the United States; or,

(2) An undivided part or share of the exclusive right; or,

(3) The exclusive right under the patent within and throughout a specified part of the United States. Rev. Stat. § 4898.

A transfer of either of these three kinds of interests is an assignment, properly speaking, and vests in the assignee a title in so much of the patent itself, with a right to sue infringers; in the second case, jointly with the assignor; in the first and third cases, in the name of the assignee alone.

Any assignment or transfer, short of one of these, is a mere license, giving the licensee no title in the patent, and no right to sue at law in his own name for an infringement.

In equity, as at law, when the transfer amounts to a license only, the title remains in the owner of the patent; and suit must be brought in his name, and never in the name of the licensee alone, unless that is necessary to prevent an absolute failure of justice, as where the patentee is the infringer, and cannot sue himself.

The term " assignment " is loosely used, both by the courts and the text-book writers. It may mean the " assignment " of an interest in a patent that is a legal title, or it may mean the " assignment" of a mere license or shop right. Properly used the term means the transfer of an interest which would be within one of the above classes.

§ 88. Recording Assignments

The statute says :[1]

Every patent or any interest therein shall be assignable in law by an instrument in writing, and the patentee or his assigns or legal representatives may in like manner grant and convey an exclusive right under his patent to the whole or any specified part of the United States. An assignment, grant, or conveyance shall be void as against any subsequent purchaser or mortgagee for a valuable consideration, without notice, unless it is recorded in the Patent Office within three months from the date thereof.

If any such assignment, grant, or conveyance of any patent shall be acknowledged before any notary public of the several states or territories or the District of Columbia, or any commissioner of the United States circuit (now district) court, or before any secretary of legation or consular officer authorized to administer oaths or perform notarial acts under § 1750 of the Revised Statutes, the certificate of such acknowledgment, under the hand and official seal of such notary or other

---

[1] R. S. 4898.

officer, shall be prima facie evidence of the execution of such assignment, grant, or conveyance.

This provision applies both to patented inventions and to patent applications, but not to a future invention nor to an invention in being not yet made the subject of a patent application. But where an assignment capable of record carries with it the assignment of future improvements upon the invention of the application or patent, it will be recorded, and the record is notice to a subsequent purchaser of both the patent and any improvement thereon.[1] And any statement or notice contained in a recorded assignment puts a subsequent purchaser on his guard.[2]

Now as to the effect of the provision above quoted. Suppose I assign to you a patent and you pay me a consideration for it after you have had an examination of the records and it appears that I have a clear title, and you record the assignment. And suppose that thereafter and within the three months' limit from its execution another assignment is recorded, previously executed by me conveying the patent to another purchaser

---

[1] Mac. Pat. § 161.
[2] National v. New Columbus, 129 Fed. 114; 63 C. C. A. 616.

for value. Who owns the patent? Evidently the earlier assignment, though recorded later, holds.

If there is any doubt as to the integrity of the assignor, the proper course is to hold up the consideration in some manner until the three months' period has elapsed and then have the record search brought down to date. But even this does not protect you against possible outstanding licenses or shop rights; and it is a wise safeguard to have the assignor, in addition to acknowledging the assignment, make affidavit and append it to the assignment to the effect that there is no previous assignment, license, or shop right, or other interest conveying any interest or right whatsoever under the patent. Only a most brazen rascal will so perjure himself and add to his crime of larceny the crime of perjury.

§ 89. Matters Concerning Assignments

Certain minor matters concerning assignments should not be passed over without notice.

¶ 1. *Unconditional Assignments*

An assignment specifying no conditions or reservations is presumed to be absolute; nevertheless the assignee takes it subject to the previous acts of the assignor.[1] As stated in the preceding section, an outstanding license does not appear of record; and while it does not affect your title to the patent, it is a break in the monopoly which you are powerless to mend.

¶ 2. *Conditions and Reservations*

Courts do not favor assignments which leave the title in mid-air. Conditions and reservations which may, in the happening of some event, affect the title, do not, prior to such happening, affect the title.[2] For example, if I assign to you a patent with the reservation that you shall pay to me a certain royalty on a given date or dates, and that if you fail to make such payment, the title shall revert to me, you hold the title none the less until the same has been canceled by a positive act. So with any other such reservation. But, of course, if you sell the patent to another, he takes it subject to such reservations and their consequences.[3]

---

[1] McClurg *v.* Kingsland, 1 How. 202; 11 L. Ed. 102.
[2] Mac. Pat. § 153.
[3] *Ibid.* §§ 166–167.

¶ 3. *Joint Owners*

From what has been said it is clear that a joint owner may, if he is a common tenant, go on parceling out the patent as he pleases. Like the alleged quality of radium — that it gives out one-half its substance in a certain period, a half of what is left in a following period, and so on to infinity, so long as a joint owner keeps the fraction inside his own fraction, he may go on parceling out forever.

¶ 4. *Executors and Administrators*

Upon the death of a holder of an assignable interest in a patent, that interest passes to the executor or administrator who qualifies, and the person so qualifying may sue for infringement.[1] But it must be remembered that we are now speaking of title interests, not mere licenses.

¶ 5. *Bankruptcy*

The title to an interest in a patent passes to the trustee of the bankrupt;[2] but the trustee can sell no better title than he holds.[3]

---

[1] Rubber Co. *v.* Goodyear, 76 U. S. 788; 19 L. Ed. 566.
[2] R. S. 5046 as amended July 1, 1898.
[3] Henry *v.* Dick, 224 U. S. 1; 56 L. Ed. 645; 32 S. Ct. 364.

¶ 6. *Creditor's Bills*

While a patent may not be seized and sold upon execution, it may be reached by a creditor's bill, or by a proceeding supplementry to execution.[1]

¶ 7. *Actions to Compel Assignment*

A patent being personalty, an action may be maintained to compel an assignment.[2] It is within the power of a court of equity to deal with a patent interest much the same as with copartnership interests.[3]

§ 90. Licenses

A license carries no interest in the patent and is not recordable in the Patent Office. In the absence of express terms it is not assignable, although acquiescence in its use may establish a continuation of it in the hands of a successor in business.[4] It therefore follows that an ordinary license, carrying no provision of assignment or

---

[1] Ager v. Murray, 105 U. S. 126; 26 L. Ed. 942; Newton v. Buck, 77 Fed. 614; 23 C. C. A. 355.

[2] Gayler v. Wilder, 10 How. 477; 13 L. Ed. 504.

[3] Nat. Wire Bound Box v. Healy, 189 Fed. 49; 110 C. C. A. 613.

[4] Lane v. Lock, 150 U. S. 193; 37 L. Ed. 1049; 14 S. Ct. 78.

transmission, expires with the death of the licensee, with the dissolution of a copartnership, and with the termination of corporate existence.

§ 91. The Several Kinds of License

Like any lease, a license may be made subject to all sorts of express provisions and may arise in various ways.

¶ 1. *Express Licenses*

A license containing various provisions and limitations is known as an express license. It may be limited as to territory; it may be limited to making, or using, or selling; it may be limited to royalty provisions; it may be limited to an arbitrary period of time; to use in a specific place; to use in connection with a specific piece of work — in short, you may write into an express license any conceivable limitation or provision which is not repugnant to common sense and equity.[1] It is even the law that a monopoly in restraint of trade in the patented article may be established by license provisions fixing the price at which the patented article may be sold, or

[1] Mac. Pat. §§ 751–755.

where it may be sold, without violation of the antitrust law.¹ And the practice of selling a patented article with a license restriction which shall reach the remotest purchaser is lawful, as settled in the Button Fastener Case many years ago and now fully confirmed by the Supreme Court in the Mimeograph Case.²

¶ 2. *Implied Licenses*

Attention has already been called to the implied license which the statute gives in case of a machine or article made before patent with the inventor's knowledge or consent (§ 74). The general, fundamental proposition is this:³

To restrict the right of a purchaser of an apparatus embodying a patented invention to use it for the purpose for which it is peculiarly adapted, there must appear some express or implied agreement by which the mode or time or place of use has been limited; and this was the principle upon which the Button Fastener Case was decided. But there may be circumstances under which the sale by a patentee of one patented article

---

¹ Bement *v.* National, 186 U. S. 70; 46 L. Ed. 1058; 22 S. Ct. 747.

² Heaton *v.* Eureka, 77 Fed. 288; 25 C. C. A. 267; Henry *v.* Dick, 224 U. S. 1; 56 L. Ed. 645; 32 S. Ct. 364.

³ Edison *v.* Peninsular, 101 Fed. 831; 43 C. C. A. 479.

will carry with it the right to use another in coöperation with the first, although the thing be covered by a second patent. Thus, if the article sold be of such peculiar construction as that it is of no practical use unless it is used in combination with some subordinate part, covered by another patent to the vendor, the right to use the latter in coöperation with the former might be implied from circumstances. It is a general principle of law that a grant necessarily carries with it that without which the thing granted cannot be enjoyed. The limitation upon this is, that the things which pass by implication only must be incident to the grant, and directly necessary to the enjoyment of the thing granted. The foundation of the maxim lies in the presumption that the grantor intended to make the grant enjoyable.

The question in the case just quoted from was the right of the defendant to use the Edison light distribution system of its general installation in connection with a special installation not furnished by the Edison company. Another case will illustrate the application of the rule.[1]

Complainant sold defendant twenty-two electric locomotives for use in its tunnels in Chicago, and

[1] Thomson-Houston *v.* Illinois, 152 Fed. 631; 81 C. C. A. 473.

consented to the installation, by a third party, of electric switches, without which the locomotives could not be operated, and upon which the complainant held a patent. Subsequently defendant purchased other locomotives of another manufacture and operated the same in the tunnels in connection with the electric switches installed. The infringement complained of consisted in the use of the patented electric switches with any locomotive not made by the complainant, it being claimed that the right to use the switch was given only in connection with the complainant's locomotives. The court held: The appellee having no notice of the restriction and not having dealt for the purchase with such restriction in mind, the license that the law raises upon the transactions between the parties is as broad as if no such restriction usually entered into the dealings of complainant with the purchasing world. The sole transaction disclosed here is the sale of the locomotives to be operated without royalty restriction (express or implied) or further license in connection with the trolley switching devices — a transaction that must be held to permit use of the same devices in connection with other locomotives.

A license which may be either a general license or a shop right, according to the circumstances of employment and the nature of the case may arise between employer and employee as will be noted more fully in the next succeeding paragraph. But the same general rule applies; for it is as true of the sale of labor and skill as of the sale of machines or apparatus, that the sale must carry the enjoyment of the thing paid for.[1]

¶ 3. *Shop Rights*

One of the most frequent and perplexing problems is that of shop rights, usually growing out of the relations of employer and employee. It is a wise provision of the law which gives the employer a shop right in the inventions of his employees which are made by them in his shops and during the time he pays for and which relate to his industry.[2] Observe how disastrous the reverse of this rule would be. Suppose the hundreds of skilled mechanics in the employ of the Westinghouse companies could take out patents on the hundreds of small improvements made from day to day in those works, and that the companies had no right to use such improvements. In a short time the management would be in a hornets' nest of pestiferous litigation such as

---

[1] Mac. Pat. § 366.
[2] *Ibid.* §§ 366–368.

would near wreck the business. So it has been wisely provided that, while employees as much as employers are entitled to their own independent inventions,[1] it is equally the rule that the inventions of employees arising in consequence of such employment give the employer a shop right[2] But it is to be noted in this connection that, in the absence of an express agreement, the employment of a skilled workman which will give a shop right by implication does not give the employer any interest in the title to the patent (see § 18).[3]

§ 92. Mortgages

It is sufficient to say that a patent may be mortgaged, and that the mortgage may be recorded in the Patent Office.[4] A patent mortgage is of rare occurrence, because usually the end that is sought in a mortgage is reached by other forms of agreements.

[1] Agawam v. Jordan, 74 U. S. 583; 19 L. Ed. 177.
[2] McClurg v. Kingsland, 1 How. 202; 11 L. Ed. 102.
[3] Dalzell v. Dueber, 149 U. S. 315; 37 L. Ed. 749; 13 S. Ct. 886.
[4] R. S. 4898.

§ 93. Monopolistic Evils

In these pages somewhat has been said concerning the case of Henry v. Dick (see §§ 70, ¶1, 89, ¶6), and a bare reference has been made to the rule of the Harrow Case (§ 91) which takes the patent monopoly outside the antitrust law. Much discussion of this subject is going on — some of it wise, but most of it otherwise. It is also the fact that large corporations are in the habit of securing large numbers of subsidiary patents and putting them in cold storage to stifle competition. I append here some of the interesting cases relating to this subject.[1]

The interesting point for the engineer to note is this: Great contending forces are at work.

---

[1] Henry v. Dick, 224 U. S. 1; 56 L. Ed. 645; 32 S. Ct. 364; Bement v. National, 186 U. S. 70; 46 L. Ed. 1058; 22 S. Ct. 747; Heaton v. Eureka, 77 Fed. 288; 25 C. C. A. 267; Edison v. Peninsular, 101 Fed. 831; 43 C. C. A. 479; Thomson-Houston v. Illinois, 152 Fed. 631; 81 C. C. A. 473; Victor v. The Fair, 123 Fed. 424; 61 C. C. A. 58; Paper Bag Cases, 105 U. S. 766; 26 L. Ed. 959; Morgan v. Albany, 152 U. S. 425; 38 L. Ed. 500; 14 S. Ct. 627; National v. Hench, 83 Fed. 36; 27 C. C. A. 349; U. S. Consolidated v. Griffin, 126 Fed. 364; 61 C. C. A. 334; American v. Pungs, 141 Fed. 923; 73 C. C. A. 157; Park v. Hartman, 153 Fed. 24; 82 C. C. A. 158; Rubber Tire v. Milwaukee, 154 Fed. 358; 83 C. C. A. 336; The Fair v. Dover, 166 Fed. 117; 92 C. C. A. 43; Gen. Electric v. Winona, 183 Fed. 418; 105 C. C. A. 652; Virtue v. Creamery, 179 Fed. 115; 102 C. C. A. 413.

Wealth and industry are tending to concentration and single control and the elimination of the competition of the past; education is going on apace and the public conscience is quickening; there is a reactionary movement against the concentration of wealth and monopolistic control which may be rather vaguely defined as socialistic. But two things are evident: first, that we shall not go back to the old — we are evolving; second, we shall not go to the extreme of anarchistic socialism — we are too conservative. But change there must be; and it is the part of the engineer to do much in the wise direction of this movement. We are apt to think the politicians rule us. Not so. The men who do things rule us. The engineer does things; and the solution of many of the industrial problems of this day are his duty. At the moment I am writing these pages the Committee on Patents of the House of Representatives is marking time — pushing none of the numerous bills introduced — because that committee does not know what should be done. There is a babel of voices. Our leaders in the engineering world should know the problems of the patent law and speak from their position as men of science.

It has been my aim in writing these pages to afford some small measure of practical information to the engineer, and to treat the subject in a broad and comprehensive way, free from bias or prejudice. With the passing of the old inventor and the arrival of the engineer inventor a new era is before us. The patent law must be made to meet the changed conditions; but it is not so much change in the patent law that will be needed as a broader, quicker, more sensitive, more responsive attitude on the part of the courts. This is coming — faster than we are aware.

Our patent system must be preserved; it must be kept from spoliation by monopoly, and it must be kept from reactionary legislation. More than any political party, more than the patent lawyers, more than any special interest or organization, the engineers of this country should have their say and say what is needful in preserving this institution which has been so great a factor in our wonderful progress.

INDEX

(References are to Sections.)

ABANDONMENT,
    Application, § 48.
    Defeats Rights, § 32, ¶ 4.
    Failure to Claim, § 32, ¶ 4.
    How and When Arising, § 32, ¶ 4.
Adaptation,
    Patentability of, § 30, ¶ 1.
Administrator,
    Application by, § 49.
    Assignment by, § 89, ¶ 4.
Aggregation,
    Combination — Distinction, § 23.
    Nonpatentable, § 29, ¶ 6.
Allowance and Issue, § 47.
Amendment,
    After First Action, § 44.
    After Second Action, § 45.
    Delay of — Evil of, § 44.
Analogous Use,
    Nonpatentable, § 29, ¶ 9.
Anticipation,
    Abandoned Device or Experiment, § 65, ¶ 4.
    Analogous or Nonanalogous Use, § 65, ¶ 3.
    Construing Claims,
        (See Claim-Construction.)
    Claim Construction, § 65.
    Ex Post Facto Judgment, § 65, ¶ 1.
    Foreign Patent, § 65, ¶ 9.
    Foreign Use, § 65, ¶ 6.
    Infringe-if-Later Test, § 65, ¶ 10.
    Inoperative Device, § 65, ¶ 5.

INDEX

Oral Testimony — Open to Doubt, § 65, ¶ 2.
Piecemeal — Dissecting, § 63.
Prior Domestic Patent, § 65, ¶ 7.
Prior Knowledge or Use in this Country, § 32, ¶ 1.
Prior Patent or Publication, § 32, ¶ 2.
Prior Patent or Publication more than Two Years, § 32, ¶ 2.
Prior Publication, § 65, ¶ 8.
Public Use, § 65, ¶ 2.
Public Use more than Two Years in this Country, § 32, ¶ 3.
Sale more than Two Years in this Country, § 32, ¶ 3.
Search — Does Not Prove Nonexistence, § 39.

Application,
    Abandoned — Renewal, § 48.
    Abandonment or Forfeiture, § 48.
    Action and Amendment after first Action and Amendment, § 45.
    Amendment or Argument after First Action, § 44.
    Claims — Required, § 41, ¶ 4.
    Data for Attorney, § 40.
    Delay in Making — Evils of, § 38, § 78, ¶ 5.
    Drawing — Nature of, § 40, § 41, ¶ 6.
    Drawings — Preparation of, § 40.
    Examination of, § 42.
    Examination — Thoroughness, § 42.
    Executor or Administrator or Committee, § 49.
    Filing of — When, § 38.
    First Action, § 43.
    Oath — Importance, § 41, ¶ 5.
    Parts of, § 41.
    Petition, § 41, ¶ 1.
    Power of Attorney, § 41, ¶ 2.
    Specification — Contents, § 41, ¶ 3.
    Terms of — Limit Claim, § 64, ¶ 2.

Applications,
    Numbers Becoming Patents, § 2.

Arrangement,
    Patentability, § 30, ¶ 5.

INDEX

Art,
    Infringement of, § 71, ¶ 1.
Article of Commerce,
    Nonpatentable, § 24.
Article of Manufacture,
    Illustration, § 24.
Art or Process,
    Definition, § 25.
Assignment,
    Action to Compel, § 89, ¶ 7.
    Bankruptcy, § 89, ¶ 5.
    Conditions and Reservations, § 89, ¶ 2.
    Creditor's Bills, § 89, ¶ 6.
    Executor or Administrator, § 89, ¶ 4.
    General Statement — Legal Title, § 87.
    Joint Owners, § 89, ¶ 3.
    Recording — Effect of, § 88.
    Recording — Statutory Provisions, § 88.
    Title — Difficulty of Determining if Clear, § 88.
    Unconditional, § 89, ¶ 1.
Assignor and Assignee,
    Infringement by, § 69, ¶ 4.
Attorney,
    Associate, § 37.
    Charges — Proper Basis, § 37.
    Duty of — To Avoid Litigation, § 21.
    Duty of — To Prevent Litigation, § 37.
    Personal Touch with, § 37.
    Power of — Nature of, § 41, ¶ 2.
    Relation to Engineer, § 4.
    Selection of, § 37.
Attorneys and Solicitors,
    Difference, § 36.

Bankruptcy,
    Assignment to Trustee in, § 89, ¶ 5.
Barbed Wire Patent,
    Cut of Drawings, § 34, ¶ 5.

INDEX

Beneficial Uses,
    Inventor Entitled to all, § 60.

CARRYING FORWARD,
    Patentability, § 30, ¶ 2.
Change of Form,
    Patentability, § 30, ¶ 3.
Chemistry,
    Chemical Engineering — Europe in Advance, § 65, ¶ 8.
Claims,
    Amendment of, § 44.
    Broadened by Reissue — Invalid, § 51.
    Failure to Claim — Illustration, § 64, ¶ 2.
    Scope of — Patent Office Indifferent if too Narrow, § 35.
    Statutory Provision, § 54.
    Vital Part of Patent, § 54.
Claim-Construction,
    Analysis of Claim, § 57.
    Anticipation, § 65.
        Abandoned Experiment, § 65, ¶ 4.
        Analogous or Nonanalogous Use, § 65, ¶ 3.
        Ex Post Facto Judgment, § 65, ¶ 1.
        Foreign Use, § 65, ¶ 6.
        Infringe-if-Later Test, § 65, ¶ 10.
        Inoperative Device, § 65, ¶ 5.
        Prior Domestic Patent, § 65, ¶ 7.
        Prior Foreign Patent, § 65, ¶ 9.
        Prior Public Use, § 65, ¶ 2.
        Prior Publication, § 65, ¶ 8.
    Beneficial Uses, § 60.
    Composition of Matter, § 57.
    Combinations, §§ 57, 58.
    Dissecting Claims, § 63.
    Elements, §§ 57, 62.
    General Rules, § 55.
    General Statement, § 53.
    Generic Invention, § 61.
    Improvements, § 61.

INDEX

Infringement, § 66.
    Combination, § 66, ¶ 1.
    Process, § 65, ¶ 2.
    Repairing and Rebuilding, § 65, ¶ 4.
    Valeat Quam Pereat Rule, § 65, ¶ 3.
Limitation, § 64.
    Disclaimer, § 64, ¶ 7.
    Omitting Element, § 64, ¶ 6.
    Patent Office Action, § 64, ¶ 3.
    Prior Art, § 64, ¶ 1.
    Reference Characters, § 64, ¶ 4.
    Reissue, § 64, ¶ 7.
    Terms of Application, § 64, ¶ 2.
    Unclaimed Element, § 64, ¶ 6.
    Words of Limitation, § 64, ¶ 5.
Manufacture, § 57.
Plain Intent and Meaning, § 56.
Process, § 57.
Reading in Elements, § 64, ¶¶ 1, 6.
Reference to Specification and Drawings, § 59.

Collar Button Case,
    Cuts of Drawings, § 24.
Combination,
    Aggregation — Distinction, § 23.
    Claims for, § 57.
    Claims — Omitting Element, § 64, ¶ 6.
    What Constitutes, § 58.
Commissioner of Patents,
    Powers of, § 6.
Common Law,
    Patent in Contravention of, § 12.
Composition of Matter,
    Claim for, § 57.
    Definition of, § 24.
    Illustration, § 24.
    Infringement, § 71, ¶ 4.
    Patentability, § 24.
Constitution,
    Provision for Patents, § 13.

INDEX

Contributory Infringement, § 70, ¶ 1.
Copartners,
    Infringement by, § 69, ¶ 3.
Corporations,
    Infringement by, § 69, ¶ 5.
Costs,
    Disclaimer — Must be Made to Recover, § 50.

DAMAGES,
    Recovery of — General Statement, § 80.
Design,
    Definition, § 27.
    Distinguished from Trade-mark, § 27.
    Infringement, § 71, ¶ 6.
Disclaimer,
    By Amendment, § 64, ¶ 3.
    Costs and Accountings, § 50.
    Difference from Reissue, § 50.
    Effect on Claim, § 64, ¶ 7.
    General Provision for, § 50.
    Invalid Claims — Injunction and Accountings, § 50.
    When Necessary, § 50.
Double Use,
    Nonpatentable, § 29, ¶ 9.
Drawings,
    For Application — Preparation, § 40.
    Nature and Function, § 41, ¶ 6.
    Use in Construing Claims, § 59.
Duplication,
    Nonpatentable, § 29, ¶ 7.

EMPLOYEE,
    Rights of — Property in Inventions, § 18.
Employer and Employee,
    Future Inventions — Assignability, § 83.
    Infringement by Either, § 69, ¶ 6.
    Shop Right — When Arising, § 91, ¶ 3.
    Improvement by Either — Ownership, § 18.

INDEX

Engineer,
    As Expert, § 67.
        Duty of, § 65, ¶ 2.
    Claim-Construction — Reasons for Understanding, § 53.
    Evidence as Expert — Injunctions, § 79.
    Inventions Made by — Assignment to Employer, § 83.
    Knowledge of Patent Law — Necessary to, § 3.
    Relation of — to Patents, § 3.
    Relation to Patent Attorney, § 4.
    Services of — Determining Invention, § 30.

Engineer and Attorney,
    Team Work by, § 44.

Engineering,
    Preventive — Patent Law Part of, § 5.
    Schools — Product of, § 1.

Equity Actions,
    Distinguished from Law Actions, § 76.
    Evidence in — How Taken, § 77.
    Geography of, § 77.
    New Equity Rules, §§ 73, 77.

Equivalents,
    Rules, § 62.

Evidence,
    Expert — Needless, § 77.

Executor,
    Assignment by, § 89, ¶ 4.
    Application by, § 49.

Examination,
    Novelty — Extent, § 42.

Expanded Metal Case,
    Cut of Drawing, § 25.

Experiment,
    Different from Improvement, § 38.
    Experimental Device — Abandoned, § 65, ¶ 4.
    Experimental Use — Not Public Use, § 38.

Expert,
    Evidence of, § 72.
    Province of, § 67.

INDEX

FEES,
    Final — When Payable, § 47.
Force of Nature,
    Nonpatentable, § 29, ¶ 2.
Foreign Patent,
    Advisability of Obtaining, § 52.
    Effect on Domestic Patent, § 52.
Forfeiture,
    Of Application — Renewal, § 48.
Function,
    Nonpatentable, § 29, ¶ 5.
Future Inventions,
    Property Rights in — Assignability, § 83.

GENERIC INVENTION,
    Construction of Claim, § 61.
    Infringement, § 72.
    What is, § 33.
Germany,
    Attitude Toward American Applicants, § 65, ¶ 8.

IGNORANCE,
    Infringement — Does Not Excuse, § 69, ¶ 7.
Immoral Object,
    Nonpatentable, § 29, ¶ 11.
Importation,
    Infringement by, § 70, ¶ 2.
Improvement,
    Construction of Claim, § 61.
    Infringement, § 71, ¶ 5, § 72.
    Ownership of — Employer and Employee, § 18.
    Patentability, § 26.
    Patenting Necessary — Reasons, § 20.
    Small — Importance of, §§ 20, 33.
Infringement,
    Art, § 71, ¶ 1.
    Article Made before Patent — Consent of Inventor, § 74.
    Anticipation Test, § 65, ¶ 10.
    Assignor and Assignee, § 69, ¶ 4.

INDEX

Buying without Right to Use, § 70, ¶ 4.
Chinese Copy, § 72.
Combinations, § 66, ¶ 1.
    Added Elements, § 65, ¶ 1.
    Different Combination, Same Result, § 65, ¶ 1.
    Identity, § 65, ¶ 1.
    Old Elements, New Function, § 65, ¶ 1.
Composition of Matter, § 71, ¶ 4.
Construing Claim,
    (*See Claim-Construction.*)
Contributory, § 70, ¶ 1.
Copartners, § 69, ¶ 3.
Corporations, § 69, ¶ 5.
Damages — Statutory Provision, § 76.
Different Classes of Invention, § 71.
Defenses — Anticipation, § 78, ¶ 3.
    A Word of Caution, § 78, ¶ 11.
    Fraud or Misrepresentation, § 78, ¶ 1.
    Fraud or Unfairness Against Another, § 78, ¶ 2.
    Joint Invention to Sole Applicant, or Sole Invention to Joint Applicants, § 78, ¶ 8.
    License, Release, Estoppel, § 78, ¶ 9.
    Noninvention, § 78, ¶ 7.
    Noninventorship, § 78, ¶ 4.
    Nonpatentability, § 78, ¶ 6.
    Not Guilty, § 78, ¶ 10.
    Other Various Defenses, § 78, ¶ 11.
    Public Use or Abandonment, § 78, ¶ 5.
    Statutory Provision, § 76.
Designs, § 71, ¶ 6.
Employer and Employee, § 69, ¶ 6.
General Statement and Statute, § 68.
General Observations, § 72.
Importation, § 70, ¶ 2.
Improvement, § 71, ¶ 5.
Intent — Ignorance, § 69, ¶ 7.
Joint Owners, § 69, ¶ 1.
Jurisdiction of U. S. District Courts, § 76.
License — Violation, § 70, ¶ 1.

INDEX

    Licensor and Licensee, § 69, ¶ 2.
    Machine, § 71, ¶ 2.
    Machine and Manufacture, § 71, ¶ 3.
    Manufacture, § 71, ¶ 4.
    Nature of Act, § 70.
    Process, § 65, ¶ 2, § 71, ¶ 1.
    Rebuilding, § 65, ¶ 4.
    Recovery for — What, § 68.
    Repairing, § 65, ¶ 4.
    Search — of Art, § 64, ¶ 1.
    Statutes Relating to, § 76.
    Territorial Rights, § 70, ¶ 3.
    Unpatented Inventions, § 74.
    Utility Test, § 72.
    Valeat Quam Pereat Rule, § 65, ¶ 3.
    Who May Commit, § 69.
    Wrongs Against Patents — General Statements, § 76.
Injunction,
    Power of — Enforcement, § 9.
    Power to Grant, § 76.
    Preliminary — Conditions Preventing, § 79.
        Evidence for and Against, § 79.
        Evidence of Engineer as Expert, § 79.
        Four Essentials to Granting, § 79.
        Most Efficient Remedy, § 79.
        Not a Matter of Right, § 79.
Insane Person,
    Application by Committee, § 49.
Intent,
    Infringement — Does not Excuse, § 69, ¶ 7.
Interference,
    Nature and Object, § 46.
    Practice and Procedure — Archaic, § 46.
    Preliminary Statement — Attorney Cannot Verify, § 41, ¶ 2.
Invention,
    Act of — Effort Involved, § 29, ¶ 1.
    Beginning of — Where Known Ends, § 2.
    Combination — Known Elements, § 17.
    Concrete Side of, § 18.

INDEX

Definition — Impossible, § 16.
Design — Test of, § 27.
Field of — Passing to Engineering, § 3.
    Progress Westward, § 6.
Foundation for — Knowledge of the Known, § 2.
Generic — Art, § 25.
Keeping Record of — Reason for, § 21.
Mechanical Skill — General Distinction, § 20.
    How to Distinguish, § 21.
    Line Between Shifting, § 20.
Mental Act, § 17.
Patentable — Classes of, § 22.
    Definition of, § 16.
    Summary, § 28.
Reduction to Practice — Concrete Act, § 18.
Reinvention — Cause of, § 17.
Reinventions — Number of, § 2.
Theft of, § 38.
Twofold Character, § 18.
Visionary — Illustration, § 18.

Inventor,
    Attainments of — Must be Large, § 2.
    Modern — Trained Engineer, § 1.
    Old Type of — Passing, § 1.
Inventor and Manufacturer,
    Traditional Antipathy, § 81.

JOINT OWNERS,
    Infringement between, § 69, ¶ 1.

LAW ACTIONS,
    Distinguished from Actions in Equity, § 76.
    When Proper, § 76.
License,
    Express, § 91, ¶ 1.
    Implied, § 91, ¶ 2.
    In General, § 90.
    Nonassignable, § 90.

INDEX

Nonrecordable, § 90.
Shop Rights, § 91, ¶ 3.
Licensor and Licensee,
Infringement by, § 69, ¶ 2.
Limitation,
Of Claim,
(*See Claim-Construction.*)
Litigation,
Avoided if Possible, § 77.
General View, § 73.
Needless Prolongation, § 77.
Prevention of — Patenting Improvements, § 20.
Unnecessary — Prevention, § 5.

MACHINE,
Definition of, § 23.
Infringement, § 71, ¶ 2.
Test of — Essential Elements, § 23.
What Constitutes — Combinations, § 23.
Machine and Manufacture,
Infringement, § 71, ¶ 3.
Manufacture,
Claim for, § 57.
Definition of, § 24.
Infringement, § 71, ¶ 4.
Mechanical Skill,
Difference from Invention, § 17.
Distinguished from Invention, § 20.
Mental Conception,
Nonpatentable, § 29, ¶ 1.
Monopoly,
Evils of Unlawful, § 93.
Patent — Absolute, § 9.
Limitation by Constitution, § 13.
Old Theory, § 10.
Unlawful — Dangers from, § 7.
Mortgage,
General Statement, § 92.

INDEX

Novelty,
    Defeated by,
        Prior Knowledge of or Use by Others in this Country Before Invention, § 32, ¶ 1.
        Prior Patent or Publication, § 32, ¶ 2.
        Public Use or Sale More Than Two Years in this Country, § 32, ¶ 3.
    Evidence of,
        (See Novelty — Tests.)
    Negative Requirements of Statute, § 31.
    Reinvention Not, § 31.
    Search — to Determine, § 39.
    Statutory Requirement, § 31.
    Tests,
        Attempted Evasion, § 34, ¶ 7.
        Commercial Success, § 34, ¶ 3.
        Efficiency, § 34, ¶ 4.
        Extensive Litigation, § 34, ¶ 6.
        Extensive Use, § 34, ¶ 3.
        Last Step Rule, § 34, ¶ 5.
        Patent Itself, § 34, ¶ 1.
        Patent Office Action, § 34, ¶ 1.
        Prior Failures, § 34, ¶ 5.
        Public Acquiescence, § 34, ¶ 2.
        Use by Defendant, § 34, ¶ 8.
        Utility, § 34, ¶ 4.
    Things which Defeat, § 32.

Oath,
    Attorney Cannot Make, § 41, ¶ 2.
    Importance of, § 41, ¶ 5.
Omitting Element,
    Combination — Avoids, § 64, ¶ 6.
Operativeness,
    Inoperative Device — Not Anticipatory, § 65, ¶ 5.

Patent,
    Basis of Industry — When, § 3.

INDEX

    Contract Theory — Stated, § 11.
    Duration of, § 9.
    Expiration — Foreign Patent, § 52.
    Grant — Creates Nothing, § 12.
        Facts versus Theories, § 12.
    Granting of — Special Acts of Congress, § 14.
    Issue of, § 47.
    Letters — Contents, § 9.
    Limitation — Constitutional, § 22.
    Meaning of Term, § 9, n. 1.
    Number Issued, §§ 2, 6.
    Obtaining — General Statements, § 35.
    Protection of — Statute for, § 15.
    Pure Monopoly, § 10.
    Rights Conferred by, § 9.
    Rights Under — General, § 9.
    Right to — Not a Natural Right, § 9.
    Trivial Inventions — Small Value of, § 20.
    What Are — General Statement, § 9.
Patentability,
    Adaptation, § 30, ¶ 1.
    Aggregation — Nonpatentable, § 29, ¶ 6.
    Analogous Use — Nonpatentable, § 29, ¶ 9.
    Arrangement — Nonpatentable, § 30, ¶ 5.
    Article of Manufacture, § 24.
    Carrying Forward, § 30, ¶ 2.
    Change of Form, § 30, ¶ 3.
    Composition of Matter, § 24.
    Constitutional Requirements, § 22.
    Double Use — Nonpatentable, § 29, ¶ 9.
    Duplication — Nonpatentable, § 29, ¶ 7.
    Force of Nature — Nonpatentable, § 29, ¶ 2.
    Function — Nonpatentable, § 29, ¶ 5.
    Immoral Object — Nonpatentable, § 29, ¶ 11.
    Introductory Statements, § 22.
    Mental Conception — Nonpatentable, § 29, ¶ 1.
    Property of Matter — Nonpatentable, § 29, ¶ 4.
    Result — Nonpatentable, § 29, ¶ 5.
    Scientific Principles — Nonpatentable, § 29, ¶ 3.

INDEX

    Simplification — Nonpatentable, § 29, ¶ 8.
    Substitution, § 30, ¶ 4.
    Systems, § 30, ¶ 5.
    Things Generally Nonpatentable, § 30.
        Tests of, § 30, ¶ 6.
    Things Nonpatentable, § 29.
    Transposition of Parts — Nonpatentable, § 29, ¶ 10.

Patent Laws,
    Constitutional Source, § 13.
    Enactment and Development, § 14.
    Knowledge of — Necessary to Engineer, § 5.
    Pivotal Act — § 4886, § 15.
    Textbooks, § 5, n. 1.

Patent Office,
    Action by — Limiting Claim, § 64, ¶ 3.
        On Application, § 43.
    Business with — in Writing, § 37.
    Character of, § 6.
    Decisions of — Conflict of, § 7.
    Early History, § 6.
    Examiners — Attitude of, § 43.
    Reforms in — Needed, § 42, n. 1.

Patent Office Gazette,
    Patents Published in, § 47.

Patent Soliciting,
    Importance of Work, § 35.
    Not Engineering Work, § 35.
    Two Views of, § 36.

Patent System,
    Benefits of, § 7.
    Reform of — Needed, § 42, n. 1.
    Service, Faults, and Dangers, § 7.
    Supremacy of, § 6.

Power of Attorney,
    Revocation, § 41, ¶ 2.

Preparing Case for Attorney,
    Essentials, § 40.

Prior Art,
    Limiting Claim, § 64, ¶ 1.

INDEX

What Included in, § 64, ¶ 1.
Process,
    Chemical — Patentability, § 25.
    Claim for, § 57.
    Definition, § 25.
    Illustrations, § 25.
    Infringement of, § 71, ¶ 1.
    Mechanical — Patentability, § 25.
    Patentability, § 25.
Profits,
    How Ascertained, § 77.
    Recovery of — General Statements, § 80.
        Statutory Provision, § 76.
Property of Matter,
    Nonpatentable, § 29, ¶ 4.
Property Rights,
    Future Inventions, § 83.
    General Statements, § 81.
    Patented Inventions — Legal and Equitable Title, § 85.
        Assignability, § 85.
        Common Tenancy, § 86, ¶ 1.
        General Rules for Buying and Selling, § 86, ¶ 1.
        Jurisdiction of Courts, § 85.
        Three Divisions of Interest, § 86.
    Tenancy by the Entirety, § 86, ¶ 3.
    Territorial Rights, § 86, ¶ 2.
    Three States of Property, § 82.
    Trust Holdings, § 86, ¶ 3.
    Unpatented Inventions — Assignability, § 84.
    Wrongs Against — How Remedied, § 75.
Public Use,
    Two-Year Period — When Begins, § 38.

REDUCTION TO PRACTICE,
    Necessary, § 18.
    Should Precede Application, § 38.
    Statutory Requirement, § 19.
    Time for — Secured by Statute, § 38.
    What is — General Rules, § 19.

INDEX

Reference Characters,
    Effect on Claim, § 64, ¶ 4.
Reissue,
    Difference from Disclaimer, § 50.
    Effect on Claim, § 64, ¶ 7.
    Rules Governing, § 51.
    Scope and Purpose, § 51.
Renewals,
    Not Permitted, § 9.
Result,
    Nonpatentable, § 29, ¶ 5.

SCIENTIFIC PRINCIPLES,
    Nonpatentable, § 29, ¶ 3.
Search,
    Infringement — What and How Obtained, § 64, ¶ 1.
    Value of, § 39.
Searches and Examinations,
    General Statement, § 39.
Secret Process or Machine,
    Protection of, § 74.
Selden Automobile Patent,
    Cut of Drawings, § 23.
Shop Rights,
    How Created, § 91, ¶ 3.
Simplification,
    Nonpatentable, § 29, ¶ 8.
Solicitors,
    Failure to Draw Proper Claims — May Defeat Patent, § 32, ¶ 4.
Specification,
    Construction — General Rules, § 55.
    Contents, § 41, ¶ 3.
    Meaning of Term, § 41, ¶ 3.
    Use in Construing Claim, § 59.
State of Art,
    Foreign — Where in Advance, § 65, ¶ 8.
    General Rules for Keeping up with, § 21.
    How Secured, § 64, ¶ 1.

INDEX

Statute of Limitations,
> Recovery of Damages or Profits, § 76.

Substitution,
> Patentability, § 30, ¶ 4.

Survey,
> Field of Discussion of this Book, § 8.

Systems,
> Patentability, § 30, ¶ 5.

TERRITORIAL RIGHTS,
> Infringement of, § 70, ¶ 3.

Transposition of Parts,
> Nonpatentable, § 29, ¶ 10.

UNCLAIMED ELEMENT,
> Combinations, § 64, ¶ 6.

Unpatented Invention,
> Assignability, § 84.
> Infringement of, § 74.
> Protection of, § 74.

Use,
> Right of — by Purchase of Patented Article, § 70, ¶ 4.

Utility,
> Determining Infringement, § 72.

www.ingramcontent.com/pod-product-compliance
Lightning Source LLC
Chambersburg PA
CBHW030811230426
43667CB00008B/1164